Smoke-Filled Rooms

SMOKE-FILLED

ROOMS HAROLD LAVINE

PRENTICE-HALL, INC., *Englewood Cliffs, N. J.*

Smoke-Filled Rooms by Harold Lavine
© 1970 by Harold Lavine

13–814632–2
Library of Congress Catalog Card Number: 71–98678
Printed in the United States of America   T
Prentice-Hall International, Inc., London
Prentice-Hall of Australia, Pty. Ltd., Sydney
Prentice-Hall of Canada, Ltd., Toronto
Prentice-Hall of India Private Ltd., New Delhi
Prentice-Hall of Japan, Inc., Tokyo

For Grace Humphreys

FOREWORD
By Raymond Moley

When Robert Humphreys moved to Washington in
1949, American political management had been forced
to grapple with momentous changes in strategy and
methods. How Humphreys, in a position of responsibility and great influence, met these changes, is indicated in the pages of this book written by him and so
skillfully and sympathetically selected and edited by
Harold Lavine.

There were two technological changes destined to
revolutionize the selection of candidates and also the
means through which their causes must be presented
to the electorate. One of these was television. The other
was air travel.

Television brought with it patterns largely designed
for mass entertainment. The candidate must not only
think and speak but act. Thus, in his selection there
must be considered whether he possessed what came
to be called "charisma," a word derived from the

Greeks and used freely in the early Christian era. Its early definition was "an extraordinary power (as of healing) given a Christian by the Holy Spirit for the good of the Church."

Air travel meant that the range of campaigning, especially in a contest for the Presidency, must cover hundreds, even thousands, of miles daily. The candidate-actor must therefore be endowed with the physical qualities necessary to meet such a strain. And under the primary system this test must extend over most of the months of the year.

Moreover, poll-taking became a considerable factor in political life. It required not only the capacity to read the omens but also its use as an instrument in conducting a campaign.

All of these innovations meant the expenditure of large sums of money. Candidates fortunate in their personal means enjoyed a considerable advantage. And if they lacked the means, they had to incur obligations which had to be met if elected.

I have grave doubts whether these new factors, which so narrow the choice, produce or will produce better public servants. But they are realities which political parties and managers must face. And Humphreys was one of the first to recognize their importance.

In the early 1940s, Ralph Robey, my colleague as a contributing editor of *Newsweek,* told me about Robert Humphreys. He had met him first in the Roosevelt-Landon campaign in 1936, when Ralph was a speechwriter for the Republican candidate and Humphreys was a reporter covering the campaign. Ralph and I both realized that *Newsweek,* a latecomer in the weekly magazine field, sorely needed more knowledgeable reporting in its National Affairs department. And so in 1944, we recommended Humphreys to the management and he was employed.

That autumn, Bob Humphreys and I traveled to the West Coast together, keeping close contact with Governor Dewey, who was seeking to defeat Roosevelt's quest for a fourth term. It was Humphreys who shrewdly noted in that year certain weaknesses in Dewey's appeal which were to contribute so materially to his surprising defeat four years later. My association with Bob Humphreys at *Newsweek* led to a friendship which continued until his untimely death in 1965.

The pages in *Newsweek* over which Humphreys presided for five years—many of which he wrote himself—showed a quality of political reporting and sophistication which no other published medium possessed. This was especially marked in his recognition of the rising importance of the great organizing ability of the political labor unions in the Democratic party. At first, this was centered in the CIO's Political Action Committee (PAC) and later in the AFL-CIO Committee on Political Education (COPE).

In 1948, organized labor, spurred by its opposition to the Taft-Hartley Act, literally took over from countless local Democratic organizations the task of registering, informing and polling the rank and file of union membership, a factor which perhaps more than any other won the election for Truman. This new factor in politics was duly recorded in *Newsweek* by Humphreys. For no one else—except the union poli-

ticians themselves—pointed out the importance of
efficient work at the level of the precinct and the town-
ship and county.

My own role in all the years of my association with
Bob Humphreys was that of a professional commenta-
tor on national politics. These contributions of mine
were made in hundreds of magazine and newspaper
articles and five books. All bear the imprint of what
I learned from Bob Humphreys. Indeed, he was the
only critic who checked and strengthened what I wrote
in those books and some of the articles. My contacts
with him were continuous during his years in Washington.

How he knew so much about what was going on in
the world of politics and the extent to which he in-
fluenced major Republican decisions is abundantly
shown in this book. This is well illustrated in his account of what was done to meet the crisis occasioned
by the famous Nixon fund in 1952. The swift action
which he, along with National Chairman Summerfield, directed provided Nixon with the means of telling
his story and certainly saved the Republican ticket
from a defeat or a near-defeat.

One crisis, prudently omitted from Nixon's book,
Six Crises, was in the early months of 1956. This decisively affected Nixon's later career. In the first three
months of that year, the President, under certain anti-
Nixon influences, doubted whether the Vice-President
should be accorded a place on the 1956 ticket. Eisenhower's ambivalence was a source of mental and emo-
tional torture for Nixon, for he was totally unable to
do anything in support of his own claim. It was Len

Hall, with Humphreys at his side, who brought upon the wavering President sufficient pressure from Republican leaders over the country to resolve the issue. I know this so well because of my many contacts with Nixon at that time.

The relations between Nixon and Humphreys throughout the Eisenhower years were warm and friendly until late in 1959. At that time, for reasons unknown to me, the relationship cooled. Humphreys, who knew of my relations with and support of Nixon, never discussed the subject with me.

Shortly after Hall left the National Committee to direct Nixon's quest of the nomination, Humphreys left, too, and became director of the National Cultural Center, drawn to this no doubt by his passionate love of fine music. He had no part in the 1960 campaign.

Bob may have regretted that the vicissitudes of his early life denied him a college education. But I wonder if this would have added anything to the amazing way in which he educated himself. For what he brought to his life was hammered out on the hard anvil of experience and in what he learned far beyond politics. His understanding and appraisal of music would have served him well had he chosen a career as a critic. His wide and disciplined reading revealed its fruits in remarkable comments upon history, economics and science. Some of us at *Newsweek* were amazed and enlightened in our meetings in 1944 when he discussed the potentials of atomic fission well before the news of Hiroshima burst upon the world.

His interest in and helpfulness to less fortunate friends won him scores of lasting loyalties.

It may have been calculated, but I prefer to believe that it was his innate modesty—in all the years during which he had so much influence in politics—which caused his name to appear so seldom in the press. Anonymity, however, gave him a barrier behind which he was able to contribute so much to the decisions of the "name" people with whom he was associated. But it is singularly fortunate that he left so much of a written record to inform a new generation. That is the durable contribution of this book.

CONTENTS

INTRODUCTION:
THE MAN IN THE WINGS

Nothing in politics just happens. There is always someone who sets the stage for it, writes the dialogue, re-
hearses the actors, prompts them from the wings. True,
sometimes the play takes on a life of its own; the actors
begin to ad-lib, the scenery collapses, the audience
joins in the action. Politics, like war, is a highly un-
certain art, which is understandable since politics is
a form of war, as war is a form of politics, a contest
for power and privilege, though by different means.
However, politics resembles war in another way: Just
as every general needs a staff as well as combat officers,
so does every political organization need a man like
Robert Humphreys.

Except for a brief interlude, Humphreys worked for
the Republican party from 1949 until his death in
1965. Almost every correspondent in Washington
knew him and knew him well, and the same is true of
almost every political reporter in the United States.
And yet, strangely, only a handful of intimates had

more than a faint idea of what his true role in the party was. They knew him as a press agent for the GOP, as a sometime campaign manager, as the director of a school for party workers, as the producer of the "Ev & Charlie Show." Most of all they knew him as a former Washington correspondent himself to whom they could go for a detailed, cold-blooded analysis of any political contest they were covering. What they didn't know was Humphreys' own role in the contest. They reviewed the play without knowing that Humphreys was both author and director.

That was the way he wanted it. Humphreys did not have "a passion for anonymity." Yet, on the other hand, he believed that his value to his party would be vastly diminished if the correspondents knew of his part in the stories they were covering. He once said: "That's what ruined Charley Michelson [the great Democratic press agent of the first Roosevelt Administration]. Once the correspondents began to understand how Michelson was operating, they began to expose him. They even credited him with things he didn't do. And that finished him."

Not the least of the reasons was a fact known to anyone who has ever ghostwritten a book or a speech: Those who employ ghosts do not relish the idea of everyone knowing they are McCarthys named Charles.

Thanks to Humphreys' steadfast insistence on remaining in the wings, hardly a word has ever been written about it, but the fact remains that, except for him, much of the history of the past two decades might never have occurred. Except for him, for example, it's unlikely that Harry S Truman would have dis-

2

missed Douglas MacArthur from his Far Eastern Command, at least when he did.

Humphreys didn't plan it that way, of course; the play took on a life of its own, and Mr. Truman refused to follow Humphreys' script.

The war in Korea was not going well. MacArthur's brilliant landing at Inchon on September 15, 1950, had shattered the North Korean forces, driving them across the 38th Parallel, but then, dizzy with success, MacArthur had ordered his armies to cross the Parallel and to occupy all North Korea. At this, Communist China entered the war. The Chinese Reds swarmed across the Yalu River into North Korea and drove MacArthur's armies into headlong retreat. Soon they were fighting simply to maintain a beachhead in South Korea.

MacArthur pleaded with Washington to let him strike back by hitting Red China itself, by bombing Red China from the air and by using Chiang Kai-shek's army on Formosa both to reinforce his own armies in South Korea and to invade the Chinese mainland. The idea appalled Washington. It appalled the nations that were fighting side by side with the Americans, under MacArthur's command, even more. They feared that Soviet Russia would come to Red China's aid. This would mean World War III.

Humphreys was then public relations director for the Republican Congressional Campaign Committee. Joseph W. Martin, Jr., of Massachusetts was the Republican leader in the House. Humphreys wrote a speech for Martin to deliver at a dinner of the Kings County Republican Committee at the Towers Hotel in

3

Brooklyn on February 12, 1951, calling on the Truman Administration to let Chiang Kai-shek "open a second front in Asia."

In simple fact, the speech was based on several misapprehensions. Humphreys, for example, accepted the estimate that Chiang had 800,000 troops on Formosa, troops who could be used to invade the Chinese mainland. Actually, Chiang's entire force—soldiers, sailors, airmen and marines—totalled only about 500,000. Of these, the Gimo had only about 30,000 to spare for combat against the Chinese Reds, and he wanted to send them not against the mainland but to Korea.

As a Pentagon general more knowledgeable than Humphreys quipped: "Unleashing Chiang would be like unleashing a Chihuahua in a lion's den."

Humphreys did not know this, and the speech he wrote for Martin was full of pyrotechnics: "What could be sounder logic . . . than to allow the anticommunist forces of the Generalissimo on Formosa to participate in the war against the Chinese Reds? Why not let them open a second front in Asia?"

Whether or not the speech was sound, as the 1952 presidential campaign later demonstrated, Humphreys had struck on a perfect issue for the Republicans. He followed up the speech by writing a letter for Martin asking MacArthur to comment on the speech. After MacArthur answered the letter Humphreys wrote another speech for Martin to deliver on the floor of the House, revealing the contents. MacArthur had written that he agreed fully with Martin on "the utilization of the Chinese forces on Formosa. . . ." He then had added in words calculated to give every European nation with forces in Korea apoplexy: "It seems strangely difficult for some to realize . . . that here we fight Europe's war with arms while the diplomats there still fight it with words; that if we lose the war to Communism in Asia, the fall of Europe is inevitable, win it and Europe probably would avoid war and yet preserve freedom. As you point out, we must win. There is no substitute for victory. . . ."

The result was MacArthur's dismissal.

Later, it was Humphreys who got the idea of inviting MacArthur to address a joint session of Congress and of having both houses of Congress hold a joint investigation of MacArthur's firing.

Historians will argue endlessly over Mr. Truman's conduct of the war in Korea and his dismissal of MacArthur, but no student of politics can deny that, by leading Martin to make the issue a basic Republican issue, Humphreys set the stage for Dwight David Eisenhower's explosive promise in the midst of the 1952 campaign: "I shall go to Korea." Not surprisingly, Humphreys also played a major role in persuading Mr. Eisenhower to make that promise.

Emmet John Hughes wrote the speech, but, as Mr. Eisenhower reported in a footnote in his memoirs, the idea came originally from Harry F. Kern, then Foreign Affairs editor of *Newsweek*. As Kern recalls what happened: "Foster [John Foster Dulles] came to dinner one night, and we started discussing the Korean War. The problem was: What should Eisenhower say about it? I came up with the suggestion that he simply say that he would go to Korea, make an on-the-scene inspection, and then decide what to do about the problem. The American voter would trust him to make the right decision.

"Foster seized on the suggestion and spent the rest of the night discussing it. He was still discussing it when I accompanied him on the elevator to his car waiting downstairs. When I got back upstairs, I called Bob in Washington and told him about my conversation with Foster. He jumped at the idea, too, and said he'd speak to Foster about it the first thing in the morning. What happened is history."

What happened was that Humphreys did speak to Dulles, and Dulles to Mr. Eisenhower. The candidate didn't need much persuading.

Humphreys was public relations director of the Republican National Committee during the 1952 campaign, but, as the above indicates, he was much more. Actually, it was he who drew up the plan for the campaign. He also drew up the plans for the 1956 and '58 campaigns after becoming campaign director of the Republican National Committee. Until Humphreys, no one had ever drawn up a formal campaign plan, and this contribution of his to political strategy became the subject of a case study by Stanley Kelley, Jr., of the Brookings Institution, in his book, *Professional Public Relations and Political Power*.

During the '52 campaign, panic struck the Republican high command over the disclosure of "the secret Nixon fund." Here, again, Humphreys played an historic part. He wasn't alone among the Republican professionals to remain calm. Many of the others did, too, notably Arthur E. Summerfield, the Republican National Chairman. However, Mr. Eisenhower was surrounded by amateurs, and Mr. Eisenhower was an amateur, himself.

It was nip-and-tuck for a time whether Mr. Eisenhower would drop Richard M. Nixon from his ticket. From the first, while others jittered, Humphreys considered the whole idea ridiculous. He argued that dropping Mr. Nixon would simply wreck the campaign and insure the election of Adlai Stevenson.

He finally came up with the idea of having Nixon deliver a speech explaining the funds. After he suggested it, Mr. Eisenhower asked him to write the speech for the vice-presidential candidate. This is the only time on record that Humphreys refused to become a ghost. He insisted the speech would never come off unless Mr. Nixon told his own story in his own words. No one could tell it for him and make it convincing.

As events proved, Humphreys was right. The most experienced and unabashed writer of soap opera could never have written what history knows as "the Checkers speech."

The Checkers speech was not the end of the episode. The full story is known by only a few men (including, of course, Mr. Nixon himself), but, after delivering the speech, Mr. Nixon became so exasperated by Mr. Eisenhower's delay in coming to his support that he decided to quit the race. Having just prevented one disaster, Humphreys found himself faced with another: Through Art Summerfield, and with the help of the vice-presidential candidate's political advisor, Murray Chotiner, he finally calmed Mr. Nixon.

All this is a matter of record. The records are in the files that Humphreys left to his widow Grace. Humphreys kept voluminous files. He kept carbons of letters that he wrote as a teen-ager and letters that he wrote to his brother Dick (the late president of Cooper Union) while he was a student at the Columbia School of Journalism. He kept records of the bets he made on elections. (Sometimes, in the course of a single week, he would make bets on a gubernatorial election in California, a senatorial election in New York, a congressional election in Indiana and a mayoralty election in Michigan. He didn't win them all, but he won far more than he lost.)

When Humphreys wrote a speech, he almost always kept a carbon, if not the original. When he attended a meeting, he made notes and filed them. One of his closest friends was Alf M. Landon, whom he covered during the 1936 campaign. Over the years after that, he and Landon exchanged hundreds of letters discussing Republican problems. They're all in the files, too, what he wrote to Landon and what Landon wrote to him.

Humphreys also was a great memo writer. He thought a great deal about the art of politics from both a philosophic and a technical standpoint. In his files is a philosophical treatise on the drift from "classic liberalism to Marxist statism" that he wrote for President-elect Eisenhower in 1952. Entitled, "Policy, Man Power and Political Action," it bears a notation in Humphreys' writing: "Carried by Eisenhower to Korea in 1952 and read in 2 sittings en route." In his files also are discussions of such matters as when and how to use billboards in a political campaign.

Many will disagree with Humphreys' political

philosophy. (Many of his closest friends did; they engaged in shouting matches with him, yet remained his friends.) No one who reads his files can doubt that he was the master political technician of his time. Most of his technical innovations are now taken for granted —including visual aids, TV-radio spots and motion pictures—but they dazzled political commentators when he first introduced them. Charles Lucey, then of the Scripps-Howard Newspaper Alliance, credited these innovations with putting new life in the Republican party. Stewart Alsop, in a *Saturday Evening Post* article on Leonard W. Hall, then Chairman of the Republican National Committee, described Humphreys as Hall's "brilliant idea man." He credited Humphreys with "converting Hall to the new style of political salesmanship. . . ."

"Humphreys showed Hall what simple ideas could accomplish politically," Alsop wrote. "It was Humphreys' idea, for example, to have a photographer on tap at all times. Thus a Republican Representative could always have his picture taken gratis, with a visiting politician, actress, performing animal or whatnot. The picture would be sent to all the newspapers in the Representative's district, and it would quite often land on the front pages. For a lowly House member, getting his picture on the front page, even in the act of shaking hands with a chimpanzee, is like striking oil. . . ."

Humphreys' files, in effect, are a textbook on modern American politics. The chapters that follow give only a sampling of them. They were not chosen at random but to give a broad spectrum of how a political technician operates and thinks. Among them is the

9

plan that Humphreys drew up for the 1952 campaign, a plan that has been seen by, at most, two dozen people until now; among them also is his account of how close Mr. Nixon came to being an ex-candidate for the Vice-Presidency and an ex-politician. The chapters include Humphreys' evaluation of businessmen in politics, his study of how labor operates in politics, his analysis of what basically is wrong with the Republican party. They were chosen specifically to present a politician's guide to politics.

They are, admittedly, one man's view. And what manner of man was he?

Physically, he was fairly slight, dark, with a small, sharp face and darting eyes. He seemed made of springs, and he could have been: One of his favorite amusements was to stand with his back to the pool table at The Players in New York, a club to which he belonged for many years, leap up, and land on the top of the table. He was excellent at pool, excellent at golf, excellent at tennis; in fact, he was good enough at tennis to play frequently with Sarah Palfrey (and even with Big Bill Tilden, who trounced him). His true passion was for excellence.

He was a serious student of baseball, but he was also a serious student of music. He could discuss music on equal terms with professors of music, which, in fact, several of his friends were. He did volunteer work to support the National Symphony Orchestra, the Howard University Choir, the Air Force Symphony Orchestra, the Kansas City Symphony, the Children's Theater in New York and the Little Theater in Indianapolis. He was a pioneer in the development of high fidelity and served on the board of directors of the International High Fidelity Stereophonic Music Festival.

He had a mind that worked with startling rapidity and sometimes with more accuracy than a computer. Those who saw the TV network computers boggle on Election Night 1968 should have seen Humphreys on Election Night 1948. Within minutes after the returns started coming in from the Midwest, he said: "Something's wrong." He sat down before a phone, called a few friends in the Midwest, stood up and told his staff: "Go home, get some sleep, and be back early in the morning. We're going to have to start writing again." It had taken only a few scattered returns from the Midwest for him to figure out, on the basis of what he knew about past elections, that Mr. Truman was going to defeat Thomas E. Dewey. It was a spectacular performance that no one who was there will ever forget.

His tolerance for views that conflicted with his own amounted almost to a religion. He sought out people with conflicting opinions. At *Newsweek,* he once hired a man who previously had been assistant managing editor of *PM,* a newspaper with a merited reputation for being far Left. A friend complimented him on hiring a man "despite the fact that he worked for *PM.*" Humphreys replied: "I didn't take him on the staff despite the fact that he worked for *PM;* I took him on *because* he worked for *PM.* I know my prejudices. I wanted someone around who could argue with me and keep me from going overboard."

One reason Humphreys could think like this was that he automatically separated a man's politics from

11

the man himself. He detested Harry S Truman's politics, for example, but he admired Harry S Truman the man. And he could become lyrical talking about Harry S Truman the politician. Harry S Truman the Democrat? That was another story.

His own basic political views can be stated quite simply: He was a Republican. He might have an intense dislike for a candidate the Republican party offered; he still didn't hesitate to work for the man. He might disagree with a position the party took; he still would help to promote it. Joe Martin was a great friend of his, and he grieved when Charles A. Halleck ousted Martin as House Republican leader. Nevertheless, he went to work for Halleck as loyally as he'd worked for Martin. He believed the nomination of Barry Goldwater in 1964 would be "a disaster." Those were his exact words. His own preference for the nomination was Nelson Rockefeller. Yet, when Goldwater beat Rockefeller for the nomination, he drew up a campaign plan for Goldwater.

He believed in the two-party system and that, if a man belonged to a party, it was his duty to fight within the party and to accept the majority will. Any other course, he felt, would mean the disintegration of the system.

By many of the liberal yardsticks, he was a "reactionary." He was militantly anticommunist. He did not agree with everything the House Committee on Un-American Activities, the Senate Internal Security Subcommittee, and Joseph R. McCarthy did, but he believed that, by and large, they were performing a useful service. On the other hand, long before the liberals discovered civil rights, Humphreys was a one-man civil rights movement. As far back as 1947, for example, he fought to hire a Negro girl for the staff of *Newsweek*. The magazine now scours the nation's colleges for Negroes, but, in those days, almost everyone on the staff, including the liberals, considered Humphreys an eccentric and told him to forget about it.

Robert Humphreys was born on July 30, 1905, in Greensville, Ohio, of Welsh, Scottish and Dutch extraction. (He looked more Welsh than anything else.) He was educated in the public schools there and in Jackson, Michigan, and Martinsville, Indiana, which he considered home. Later, he spent a year at Columbia studying journalism.

He started his newspaper career as a reporter for the Houston Press in 1931. A year later, he started his political career as publicity director of the Indiana Republican State Central Committee. After that, for years, until he joined the Republican Congressional Campaign Committee, he alternated between journalism and politics.

If truth be told, even as a journalist, Humphreys could not resist dabbling in politics. As Capitol Hill correspondent for International News Service, for example, he scored many a beat on the work of the House Committee on Un-American Activities simply because he gave the staff members of the committee so many leads.

He became executive news editor of INS in Washington and then, in 1944, joined *Newsweek* as Na-

13

tional Affairs editor. At *Newsweek,* still a man deeply concerned with politics, he ran a story promoting Mr. Eisenhower for President as early as 1947.

After Dewey's defeat in 1948, a group of House Republicans, headed by Joe Martin, asked him to confer with them in Washington. They were dissatisfied with the work the Republican National Committee had been doing in promoting the party. They wanted to establish a new publicity organization with Humphreys in charge.

He was reluctant. He had a top job at *Newsweek,* with a good chance of some day becoming editor. Martin and the others kept after him. Finally, after four months, he relented, becoming publicity director of the Republican Congressional Campaign Committee.

Later, he became publicity director of the Republican National Committee and, still later, campaign director. In January 1960, he quit to become staff director of the National Cultural Center. His love of music had overcome his love of politics.

However, he could not stay away from politics long. By March 1961, he was back as staff director of the Joint Senate and House Republican Leadership.

One day, playing tennis, he felt a sharp pain. He went to a doctor, who discovered that he was suffering from cancer. It proved fatal.

At his funeral, the late Republican leader of the Senate, Everett Dirksen, delivered the eulogy. Every Republican politician mourned. And so did everyone who had known Robert Humphreys, regardless of what side of the political fence he was on.

EPH W. MARTIN, JR.
TH DIST. MASSACHUSETTS

Office of the Minority Leader
House of Representatives
Washington, D. C.

March 8, 1951

PERSONAL

My dear General:

In the current discussions on foreign policy
and overall strategy many of us have been distressed that although
the European aspects have been heavily emphasized we have been
without the views of yourself as Commander-in-Chief of the Far
Eastern Command.

I think it is imperative to the security of
our nation and for the safety of the world that policies of the
United States embrace the broadest possible strategy and that
in our earnest desire to protect Europe we not weaken our position
in Asia.

Enclosed is a copy of an address I delivered
in Brooklyn, N.Y. February 12, stressing this vital point and
suggesting that the forces of Generalissimo Chiang Kai-Shek
on Formosa might be employed in the opening of a second Asiatic
front to relieve the pressure on our forces in Korea.

I have since repeated the essence of this
thesis in other speeches and intend to do so again on March 21
when I will be on a radio hookup.

I would deem it a great help if I could have
your views on this point, either on a confidential basis or otherwise.
Your admirers are legion and the respect you command is enormous.
May success be yours in the gigantic undertaking which you direct.

Sincerely yours,

Joseph W. Martin Jr.

General of the Army Douglas MacArthur
Commander-in-Chief
Far Eastern Command

Tokyo, Japan.

20 March 1951.

Dear Congressman Martin:

I am most grateful for your note of the 8th forwarding me a copy of your address of February 12th. The latter I have read with much interest, and find that with the passage of years you have certainly lost none of your old time punch.

My views and recommendations with respect to the situation created by Red China's entry into war against us in Korea have been submitted to Washington in most complete detail. Generally these views are well known and clearly understood, as they follow the conventional pattern of meeting force with maximum counter-force as we have never failed to do in the past. Your view with respect to the utilization of the Chinese forces on Formosa is in conflict with neither logic nor this tradition.

It seems strangely difficult for some to realize that here in Asia is where the Communist conspirators have elected to make their play for global conquest, and that we have joined the issue thus raised on the battlefield; that here we fight Europe's war with arms while the diplomats there still fight it with words; that if we lose the war to Communism in Asia the fall of Europe is inevitable, win it and Europe most probably would avoid war and yet preserve freedom. As you point out, we must win. There is no substitute for victory.

With renewed thanks and expressions of most cordial regard, I am,

Faithfully yours,

DOUGLAS MacARTHUR.

Honorable Joseph W. Martin, Jr.,
House of Representatives,
Washington, D.C.

This draft of a statement for the Speaker of the House bears the following, hastily scrawled, identification: "9 AM conference in Speaker [Joseph W.] Martin's office morning after McArthur (sic) was fired attend by Sens. [Robert A.] Taft, [H. Styles] Bridges, [William F.] Knowland and [Owen] Brewster, Cong. [Charles A.] Halleck, [Edwin Arthur] Hall, and [Dewey] Short. This press statement issued at 11 AM by Martin [was] written by RH who [was the] only outsider present."

[handwritten draft:]

9 AM conference in Speaker Martin's office morning after McArthur was fired attend by Sens. Taft, Bridges, Knowland and Brewster, Cong. Halleck, Hall, and Short. this press statement issued at 11 am by Martin was written by RH who only outsider present.

SPEAKER'S OFFICE

the conference was agreed:

1. That the whole question and inability of the conduct of foreign policy be investigated must be by Congress.

2. That the Congress should have the complete views of Gen MacArthur and he should be invited to return for that purpose forthwith.

In addition the question of possible impeachment of the President was discussed at length. No decision was reached.

OFFICE OF THE VICE PRESIDENT

WASHINGTON

July 12, 1956

Dear Bob:

This is just a note to tell you how
much Pat and I appreciated your taking the
time and trouble to welcome us home at the
airport yesterday.

Since we were away such a short
time, we were really overwhelmed to see so
many of our friends when we stepped out of
the plane. In fact, we both felt that our reception was the highlight of the entire trip, and
you certainly have our gratitude for helping
to make it so.

With kindest regards,

Sincerely,

Richard Nixon

Mr. Robert Humphreys
Republican National Committee
1625 Eye Street, N. W.
Washington 6, D. C.

January 8, 1960

Dear Bob:

As you leave your post as Campaign Director, I want
to take this opportunity to express my deep appreciation for
your dedicated service to the Republican Party during your
tenure in a most sensitive and difficult job.

May I add, too, how much I personally have appreciated
the wise counsel and loyal support that you have given to me
through the years. I remember those discouraging days in
the Hiss case when you took Bob Stripling and me to New York
and introduced us to Bill Conklin, Tom O'Neill and a couple
of the other key reporters who were covering the trial. And,
of course, I shall always be grateful for the way you stood by
me during the famous fund controversy of the 1952 campaign.

I know that with your background in music you will enjoy
the challenging opportunity of directing the campaign for funds
for the new Cultural Center. I will welcome the opportunity
to be of any assistance I can in this very worthwhile and
historic enterprise.

With every good wish,

Sincerely,

Richard Nixon

Mr. Robert Humphreys
108 Sangamore Road
Mt. Sumner Hills, Maryland

I

THE STORY OF "DOCUMENT X"

Early in the morning of August 2, 1952, a man walked into the elevator of the Brown Palace Hotel in Denver. He was carrying an armful of flipboards of the kind advertising men use to make presentations. He said, "Basement, please." Humphreys walked into the basement, built a fire in the boiler of the hotel, and burned the flipboards one by one. He previously had made three copies, book size, one for Eisenhower, one for Summerfield and one for himself. To the handful of Republicans who have ever read them, perhaps two dozen in all, they still are known as "Document X."

They are the blueprints for Eisenhower's 1952 campaign.

It was Humphreys who drew up the blueprints. Until he did, no one in the whole history of U. S. politics had ever actually planned a campaign. Whether a man was running for alderman or mayor or governor or President, he started off with a general idea of what he would do and then improvised. Humphreys, who had a quick mind, was a master at improvisation; but he also had a very tidy mind, and he, therefore, also believed in having a master plan to improvise on. "Document X" was his first master plan. He later drew up others. Since Humphreys, drawing blueprints for a campaign has become standard in U. S. politics.

In January 1959, Sherman Adams wrote Humphreys asking him for his recollections of the 1952 campaign. A long correspondence developed, covering not only "Document X" but a great many other aspects. In his first letter to Adams, dated January 14, 1959, Humphreys wrote: "I am only going to answer one of your questions in this letter . . . I am going to cover your inquiry regarding the Brown Palace presentation of the 1952 campaign plan." He presented the plan—the day before he burned the flipboards—at a conference with Eisenhower and several of Eisenhower's advisors in the Brown Palace; and he wrote:

My recollection is that there were nineteen people present, but I have only my memory as to who they were—no records.

They were: General Eisenhower, Senator Nixon, Senator Lodge, Governor Adams, Senator Carlson, Arthur Summerfield, Sinclair Weeks (?), Senator Dirksen (?), Congressman Hall, Walter Williams (?), Mrs. Lord (?), Jim Hagerty, Tom Stephens, Arthur Vandenberg, Jr., Fred Seaton (?), Murray Chotiner, Robert Mullen (?), James Ellis (President of Kudner Agency), Wes Roberts, Wayne Hood and me.

This adds up to 21.

I have put question marks after several of the names

because I am not positive they were present. For example, I don't know if Fred Seaton was yet on the scene or not, and I have a vague idea Dirksen had to leave before the meeting that night.

There is also the possibility that Jim Hagerty had an assistant present, a Kansas editor whose name escapes me.

The presentation took forty minutes to make and, as I recall, the General sat in the middle of the first row with Cabot Lodge on his left. I recall distinctly that Cabot, at the conclusion of the presentation, was immediately given the floor on the ground that he had to catch a plane that night and must leave within the hour. Cabot was the most vocal person in the room in his comments on the plan. I have no recollection of his opposing it on any ideological basis. I do recall that he had a very forthright set of ideas about use of television and rallies because he and I got into quite a discussion about it and at one point I recall Arthur Summerfield joining in, but mostly the give and take was between Cabot and myself.

Incidentally, I do not recall General Eisenhower saying a single word during the evening once the presentation had been made. Judging by the absence of much comment, other than by Cabot, we felt the plan, on the whole, had general acceptance in the room.

Cabot contended that we should abandon political rallies because people would not go to them if the event were on TV. He argued that when the General made a speech for broadcast purposes we should use theater-size auditoriums because (and I am not sure these are his exact words, but it is the thought behind

17

his words) "we'll have trouble filling the hall." I contended that TV would have no impact detrimental to political rallies and pointed out that while the campaign plan strongly urged both the President and Vice-President to use "informal intimate television productions addressed directly to the individual American and his family, their problems and their hopes," we by no means felt that political rallies should be avoided but, on the contrary, made even bigger.

You can believe it or not, this discussion lasted quite a few minutes.

Some idea as to the ultimate outcome can be gained from the fact that when we finally opened the campaign in Philadelphia for the President's first nation-wide TV broadcast the crowds at the rally broke all records in Convention Hall. The thoroughly-frightened fire marshal estimated at 6:00 P.M. (broadcast time was 9:30) that 20,000 people were jammed into an arena seating 14,000 (they couldn't even get the doors closed) while Philadelphia police, facing the worst traffic in the city's history, estimated 60,000 were turned away. For example, Delaware organized a fifteen-car special train from Wilmington to take them to Philadelphia and the traffic jam was so terrific they couldn't get on the siding near Convention Hall to unload their passengers and they went home without ever getting to the rally.

The presentation was made on large flipboards (advertising-agency style) and I personally built a fire in the Brown Palace boiler the next morning and burned the boards one at a time until they were all completely destroyed. Three bound reductions of the boards in

18

book size were retained—one for the President, one for Art Summerfield and I have the other.

The presentation was made on the night of July 30 (I remember because it is my birthday). As I recall, Vice-President Nixon, Arthur Summerfield, Murray Chotiner, Wayne Hood, Wes Roberts and I flew in from Columbus, Ohio (where Nixon and Summerfield addressed the Ohio Republican State Convention in an ameliorating move toward the Taft people), arriving in Denver at approximately 1 or 2 o'clock. We were immediately rushed to the Brown Palace and into an extremely lengthy room where all the Brown Palace-Ike staff, plus Citizens' people—altogether I would say 35 or 40 people—sat around a long table awaiting a pep talk from the General, the campaign plan presentation following that event about 8:30 or 9:00.

The plan was complete from stem to stern.

It was divided into six sections, the first dealing with basic strategy . . .

The first half of the section on basic strategy . . . dealt with the necessity of reuniting the "hard-core vote of 20 million Republicans." The plan argued that this was the hard core and had been split asunder by the Eisenhower-Taft struggle. Therefore, the first task was to get the Taft people back in line. From that point it argued that 20 million votes were not enough and raised the question of where to find the additional votes.

As you recall, we had complete campaign tours laid out in the plan, together with maps, and these were followed almost to the letter with two exceptions. These exceptions were:

19

1. The campaign plan said nothing about the pre-campaign Southern two-day tour. I understand this was solely the President's idea. The first time we knew anything about it at National Headquarters was when you or Fred Seaton started talking to us on the phone. For your further information, it was not highly applauded in the Washington Headquarters at that time. This was probably our first lesson in the fact that the President undoubtedly had better political instincts than any of us because by the time he had made his first two steps in that two-day swing, we knew we had been dead wrong in looking on it with a fishy eye. Either you or Seaton told me one time that the President insisted on doing this because he "promised those people" that he would visit their states during the campaign and he was determined to live up to his promises. That may not be all the story, but it is all I know.

2. The plan called for the campaign to open in Indianapolis, Indiana, in the heart of the Taft belt. As you recall, we all remained in Denver for five days and among the subjects discussed at length during those five days was where to open the campaign. As I recall it, you took the lead in moving it away from the Midwest. I remember that one evening right after dinner, in your office, I suggested that we open in Philadelphia under the auspices of the Young Republicans. You seized on this and accepted it because up to that time we had been arguing for Indianapolis. Philadelphia it became, with YR sponsorship. One more thing which I will write you about at greater length after I gather some more facts—

20

The campaign plan had an organization chart built around the Republican National Committee and its Chairman, together with this comment:

"The Chairman of the Republican Senatorial and Congressional Committees are brought into the operations in a direct advisory capacity so that the functions which they perform can be closely integrated into the campaign effort—and still maintain the legal separation which is required under existing Federal statutes. A similar status is given the Eisenhower-for-President Clubs under the heading of 'National Volunteers for Ike.' "

This was a forthright effort to bring the Citizens for Eisenhower under the control of Summerfield and the Republican National Committee. The reason for it was a valid one—not the desire of some power-hungry people to control everything. The basic reason was the horrible memory of the botch inflicted on the 1940 campaign by the completely out-of-hand "Willkie Clubs."

As you undoubtedly recall, you spent the better part of three days refereeing this scrap and ultimately were able to take to General Eisenhower an agreement which all sides accepted. . . .

Humphreys' next letter to Adams is dated January 30, 1959.

I discovered that Wayne Hood was going to be in town this week so I delayed this letter until I had a chance to talk with him . . . Sure enough, his recollections contained some elements missing from mine.

21

For example:

Wayne said that "we"—meaning the National, Senatorial, Congressional Committee contingent—were strongly suspicious that Walter Williams was going to be made Campaign Manager. Beyond remembering the all-night session, I don't quite recall the Walter Williams angle, but Wayne was very positive about it.

If I had to reconstruct my own vague recollections on this point, they would be something along this line: That Cabot had taken himself out of the picture because of his own senatorial campaign and that a fellow named Adams seemed to be the more likely prospect. Wayne says no, that there was an idea that Walter Williams was the Adams candidate.

At any rate, at some juncture during the five-day stay, Arthur was named Campaign Manager. As you know better than I, this was frequently a difficult role he had. What we alternately called the "Denver Crowd," later changed to the "Commodore Crowd," actually had the most to say about things. As Len Hall later told me, most of those decisions were based on Eisenhower's own wishes, which we, at the Washington end, frequently did not know.

Point: I don't recall the above conflict as too serious, and didn't at the time, because it is inevitable that those immediately surrounding a candidate and those operating from a fixed position in the party structure are not always going to agree because they have different sets of facts before them—and, as you know, we didn't always agree. However, I don't recall any serious differences although later in this letter I will outline several which did approach the boiling point without any serious eruptions.

First, as to your own presence on the scene:

On Tuesday afternoon, July 15, after the Convention, I flew to Flint for emergency sessions with Art, and Len Hall arrived the next morning from a vacation spot in Montana. We stayed with Art Summerfield in his home for five days, and worked from his office putting together a National Committee headquarters staff; initial ideas for the campaign plan (discussed in my previous letter) were explored, a decision to start working on the Taft group was reached, the decision to bring Wayne Hood and Wes Roberts into the picture was made and I distinctly recall Art Summerfield, sometime late during that week, welcoming the fact that you had agreed to go to Denver, because young Vandenberg up to that time appeared to be handling the show and things were pretty sketchy.

(Incidentally, during that weekend—and you might have been the agent at the Denver end—we engineered a telegram from Eisenhower to Taft at his vacation spot in Canada. Western Union goofed on delivery. Meantime, during the same week, Taft flew to Washington for an off-record one-day meeting in his Senate office with his key people, and we, in Flint, knew through espionage that Taft had not received the telegram. We also knew that during the day he had a letter put before him for his signature to all of his delegates which was not going to help matters and we were moving heaven and earth by indirection to get it changed. . . . When the Ike telegram was finally delivered eight or ten days too late, it accomplished zero and everybody had to start all over.)

The first face-to-face meeting of the Denver and Washington wings occurred as I indicated in my previous letter, starting July 30.

Apparently there were four bones of contention in this order of intensity: (a) role of Citizens, (b) whether the General would support the Republican nominees, (c) whether the General would recognize commitments, after he became President, that might be made by the party leaders during the campaign and (d) who would be his Campaign Manager. There was also a minor skirmish going on about Art's choice of Kudner as the advertising agency, and, if I recall correctly, people from Young & Rubicam and McCann-Erickson were actually on the scene agitating that Kudner was "not big enough." I remember Sinny Weeks buttonholing me as we got off the plane about it and there were pressures right and left on the subject (you will recall after the bad TV lighting of the General at the Philadelphia opening, Jim Ellis, of Kudner—so he has told me—was handed a list of ten agencies and told to pick one which would share the account with Kudner, and he picked BBD&O).

On Citizens: This row lasted several days and your role, as I recall it, was umpire-in-chief who was trying to get an agreement that could be taken to the General. Most of the meetings were in your office. The Citizens wanted to operate completely independently, setting up their own organization and raising their own money in every state without reference to anyone in the Republican party. I believe we took the other extreme that they should be very definitely controlled by the party machinery. About the second day, the *New York Times* busted the story and we always suspected Bob Mullen of deliberately planting it—which would have been a good tactic.

These conferences in your office were invariably attended by Summerfield, Weeks, sometimes Hall, Roberts, Hood and me, with Williams, Lord, Charlie Willis and Mullen to my certain knowledge for Citizens, with you always present and frequently, Hagerty.

The agreement finally reached was that Citizens' organizations must be cleared with Wes Roberts as the "liaison man" for the National Committee. The idea was that national Citizens would give proposed names of state Citizens' leaders to Roberts and then he would attempt to work out acceptability or rejection with Republican state chairmen, et al. (Wes practically lived on the phone night and day from then on trying to accomplish this almost insuperable task.)

I recall that as we were approaching agreement, there was considerable discussion of how we could tell the press about it. At one point I served as the guinea pig to provide soothing answers to Hagerty who, posing as the antagonistic newspaperman, cross-examined me in front of the assemblage in your office. My recollection is that finally the agreement was given to the press in statement—perhaps a joint one.

I recall no agreement about the financial end of Citizens, but I do know this—Jock Whitney and Sidney Weinberg worked hand-in-glove with all of us and were very helpful on (1) exercising cooperative control through the purse strings, and (2) making sure

25

that Citizens and the Republicans stayed out of each other's way in soliciting people for contributions.

On Republican nominees: Summerfield obtained an agreement from General Eisenhower that he would support all duly nominated Republican candidates. This, as you will recall, committed him to supporting Senators Jenner, McCarthy, Malone, and Kem and several others about whom many Eisenhower supporters were not too happy.

I think the first skirmish [that] you and Art had occurred as the General's plane left Cleveland for Indianapolis early in the campaign where some doubt had arisen whether the General would endorse Jenner (he did it that night).

The next one in this connection occurred when Eisenhower went into Wisconsin. A rumor that he might endorse McCarthy, but defend Marshall in the same breath reached Summerfield and he and possibly two U. S. Senators (one of them might have been Carl Mundt) got on the Eisenhower train as it crossed Illinois into Wisconsin in the middle of the night to see if they could prevent this from happening, as they feared it would be interpreted as a slap at McCarthy. I have been told since that Sulzberger, of the *New York Times*, had sent word that the price of the *Times'* endorsement would be whether Ike defended Marshall in Wisconsin, but I do not have any firsthand knowledge of this. At any rate, as I understand it, the Marshall defense was in the Milwaukee speech, but was taken out.

On Ike's recognition of pre-election GOP commitments: Approximately August 1st or 2nd, Arthur requested and obtained a private meeting with Eisenhower to be attended only by Arthur, Wes Roberts, Wayne Hood and me. The purpose of the meeting was to get from Eisenhower an understanding that once elected he would recognize party channels for filling jobs and would realize that in a campaign, commitments for the future might have to be made. Wayne Hood was especially adamant on this point and in the all-night session preceding the meeting, to which I have already referred, had threatened to quit unless there was some satisfaction. Frankly, I don't have too much memory of *this* aspect of the meeting with Eisenhower since it was hardly in my bailiwick, but I do recall that Wayne kept pressing the point—also that he didn't quit when it was over, but stayed on during the campaign. Did you ever know anything about this?

On Campaign Manager: I have no firsthand information, nor any recollections, on this point other than that Arthur was named to the job. Perhaps you have some.

You asked my recollections about some of the skirmishes.

One skirmish I recall, because I was in it. The AFL Executive Board of fifteen members was meeting in Atlantic City. I got a mysterious phone call urging that I see a gentleman who would arrive the next morning from Atlantic City. This man walked into my office, declined to take a seat, and said he could tell me all he had to say standing up and that it would not take more than thirty seconds. Standing, he said to me that the Executive Board had voted the previous afternoon, fourteen to one, to have the AFL Conven-

27

tion endorse Stevenson—*after* both Stevenson and Eisenhower had spoken. In the entire history of the AFL, it had never endorsed a presidential candidate before and this was to be a *coup* to box Eisenhower.

When the man left, I checked over some other sources and got a partial confirmation—enough to be absolutely convinced of the veracity of what I had been told. I knew that you, Stassen and Cabot had been attempting to deal with labor leaders in an effort to work out something in the way of support for the General and I also recall that I had taken a very dim view of it. I went to Arthur's office and related all this to him. He said to me: "You know more about this than anybody else, why don't you get on the tie-line with Governor Adams?" (We had set up a tie-line between the Hotel Washington and the Brown Palace, ditto later at the Commodore.)

I told Arthur I didn't think we should phone the information until we had worked out a recommendation to go with it.

I got in touch with some labor people that I could trust and their proposition to me was to have Eisenhower take the steam out of the AFL sails by having him tell them in his speech that he knew what they were up to—and then address his message to the rank-and-file.

This seemed like pretty good strategy to us so I was commissioned to talk it over with you on the tie-line.

You were pretty rough. First—and I don't blame you—you were disbelieving about the information. You said that you had other sources of information but that you would check. I don't think I got my proposal

28

before you on the phone because I recall that I had
another session with you on the phone at my instiga-
tion trying to sell you on the idea. You weren't buying.
I was absolutely convinced that we were walking into
a cul-de-sac and I recall that I fretted for days about
it and might even have had a third conversation with
you.

I recall distinctly being in the Commodore when
the General came East to go to the Madison Square
Garden AFL Convention and trying to convince
Frank Carlson that maybe I had something, but everything had been wrapped up by that time. You will
recall that they had Eisenhower one day, Stevenson
the next day, and then endorsed Stevenson. I bled
plenty at the time. I actually doubted later that it made
a hell of a lot of difference what we did . . .

*In the course of the correspondence, Adams asked
Humphreys for further recollections of Eisenhower's
Milwaukee speech, a speech that was sensational not
because of what Eisenhower said but rather because of
what he didn't say. In the prepared text—which already had been mimeographed and distributed—Eisenhower had praised General George C. Marshall, a
target of Wisconsin's Republican Senator Joseph R.
McCarthy. When he delivered his speech, Eisenhower
omitted his words of praise. Humphreys couldn't tell
Adams why. He wasn't there. However, in his reply
to Adams, on February 19, 1959, he did contribute a
small footnote to history.*

I know one or two things about the event but I
don't think they are very important.

29

1. A great many of us felt that the General should make his major communism speech in Milwaukee and this was finally agreed to.

2. There was a great deal of jockeying about as to who should prepare the material because some of the strong anticommunists were fearful that the General might be "sold" a weak speech. I remember that I had breakfast with Clare Luce at her New York town house somewhat late in September and she told me that she had found a fellow who should write the speech, in fact, it was already written, and according to Clare, was a superb document. Her find: Emmet Hughes, a *Time* editor.

3. The Wisconsin trip did have one definite effect: It set at rest any doubt that had existed as to whether or not the General would be tough on domestic Communists and their infiltration in the Government.

As Humphreys admitted when he wrote these letters to Adams, he wrote them strictly from recollection. Adams checked everything he wrote, and found a few inaccuracies. On February 4, 1959, "Ground Hog Day Plus 2," Adams wrote Humphrey: "This is not a very important matter, but is a commentary on your recollection."

Art Summerfield's calendar, he said, showed the conference at the Brown Palace had taken place on August 1. "You say it was the evening of the 30th because it was your birthday which you haven't forgot.

30

Now maybe you had another meeting on your birthday in Ohio?"

Humphreys replied:

Again I surrender—the Summerfield-Nixon party arrived in Denver August 1 . . . the great event on July 30 was the announcement that I was public relations director, an event both the nation and I survived . . .

Another correction that Adams made in Humphreys' story: "By the way, although I think you are right 99 and 44/100th percent of the time, I think you will find that Ike spoke to the AFL at the Commodore and not at the Garden."

II

"DOCUMENT X"

Later, Humphreys was to say of "Document X" that it "made political history." This was not an overstatement. For, as Humphreys wrote, with complete justification, in a chapter he contributed to a book entitled Politics 1960, *it "probably marked the first time that any candidate—Presidential or otherwise—knew weeks ahead of the opening of his campaign what his basic strategy would be, how he would implement it, and who would be responsible for the implementation . . .*

"The advantages of advance planning for the 1952 campaign were so obvious," he wrote, "that four years later a plan for President Eisenhower's second campaign was presented to him at the White House in mid-June 1956, and likewise adopted.

"The amazing thing about these campaign plans was not their novelty but that advance planning had never been reduced to paper before."

Here, with only a few maps and a chart omitted, is the text of "Document X":

CAMPAIGN PLAN

I. Foreword.
II. Saying the things that win votes.
III. Doing the things that win votes.
IV. Where and when to say and do them.
V. Functions: Who will say, and who will do.
VI. Recapitulation.

PART I

FOREWORD

Our job can be stated simply. It is to win enough votes in enough states to elect the next President of the United States, together with enough Senators and Congressmen to afford workable Republican majorities in both branches of the Congress.

We must start with the people who are now Republicans—the 20 million voters who have stuck with the Republican party through thick and thin. *They must not be alienated.*

We must face the fact that at the moment several million of them, particularly in the Midwest, are at least bewildered. They know that the press and radio have, on the whole, interpreted the events in Chicago as a "purging" of the party. They wonder where their candidate stands. And because they believe that many

34

of those whom they have followed in the past are now out of the picture, *the situation must be regarded as serious.*

Obviously, *the first task* is the reorientation and re-integration of these several million persons in a united drive for votes.

Assuming success in this, *the question remains as to how we approach the main task of winning enough additional votes to insure victory.*

In considering this problem we must start from the premise that an intact vote of 20 million Republicans is not sufficient to win the election on November 4. This has been proven by the results of five consecutive elections.

Where can these additional votes be found?

There are two ways to answer this question.

One answer is found in the strategy which guided the campaigns of 1940, 1944 and 1948. These campaigns were based upon the assumption that the hunting ground was the so-called "independent" vote, with a collateral assumption that the best appeal to this vote was the "liberal" one.

Currently, this viewpoint is being advanced by commentators of the Alsop and Lippmann school. They say there are only three kinds of voters: Republicans, Democrats, and Independents (liberals), and that the Independents (liberals) hold the balance of power. Therefore, a winner must appeal to them.

This line of thinking was largely responsible for what the newspapers branded the "me too" campaigns of Willkie in 1940 and Dewey in 1944 and 1948.

The other answer is to say that there are four potential sources of votes instead of three. They are: Republicans, Democrats, Independents and Stay-At-Homes—*those who vote only when discontent stirs them to vote against current conditions.*

In this more realistic grouping, it is not assumed that either the Independent or Stay-At-Home vote is necessarily a "liberal" vote. A safer assumption is that both, like all other voters, are a cross-section of various political philosophies.

The pertinent fact is that the Stay-At-Homes outnumber the Independents by approximately 45 million to an estimated 3 or 4 million. They are the "agin" voters who had a great deal to do with electing Harding in 1920 and Roosevelt in 1932. Certainly they played some part in the 1946 Republican sweep which turned control of the Congress over to the GOP for two years.

PART II

SAYING THE THINGS THAT WIN VOTES

If the candidate is to retain the hard core of 20 million Republican votes, attract a substantial part of the Independent vote and stimulate the Stay-At-Homes into action in sufficient numbers to win, he must clearly state that he is against what has been going on and intends to change conditions.

There are millions of people in all voter categories who are *against* wasteful spending, *against* corruption in high places, *against* higher and higher taxes, *against* Communist fumbling in our international relations, and *against* political self-interest being placed ahead of our national interest.

It is to these voters and potential voters our appeal must be directed.

This does not preclude the candidate from standing "for" something. But it proposes to weight the campaign on the side of attack.

It does not mean "going back to 1929."

It does not mean endorsement of any controversial positions associated with the Taft forces.

The whole spirit of a campaign conducted on this level would be one which would inspire a crusading zeal that is impossible to engender by the "me too" approach, or anything which promises only to better what the present Administration is doing.

In conclusion, it should be noted that the two most recent and outstanding examples of political success based on attack were: (1) President Truman's fighting campaign of 1948, and (2) *The full-scale attack launched on the Taft forces by the Eisenhower supporters in the pre-convention and convention days of 1952.*

If the strategy of attack is adopted, it follows that the crusade must be spearheaded against those areas where the present Administration is weakest. These should be covered generally and in the broadest outline in the candidate's Speech of Acceptance in early August, and then spelled out in greater detail in eight to ten major speeches during the balance of the campaign. Suggested subjects for major speeches follow:

1. FEAR

This is a double-barreled subject.

The first aspect is that for twenty years the Democrats have deliberately fostered fears in the American people by creating and proclaiming one emergency after another, sometimes real, but mostly imagined.

The second aspect is that through its blunders the Administration has brought about an international situation that today causes Americans, who once experienced no fear other than the possibility of financial insecurity, *to fear for their national security and lives*.

The entire nation has been conditioned to a fear psychology and the American people are yearning today for an Administration which can offer them not only peace in the world, but *peace of mind*.

2. INFLATION

One of the greatest elements of insecurity among the American people today is government-sponsored inflation.

The breadth of this appeal is enormous. The housewife cannot make ends meet. Youth can see no future. Labor is chasing its tail in an endless cycle of wage increases followed by price increases which destroy their buying power.

Business finds its reserves depleted daily, and its

plans for expansion checkmated by inflationary factors over which it has no control. Insurance and retirement income steadily diminishes in value.

The farmer, historically subject to the caprice of weather, now suffers the additional burden of capricious prices.

Not a single American is untouched by the ravages of inflation, and no law yet devised by man has ever stopped inflation once it got fully under way.

The only cure is fearless and courageous executive management by Government, and all those who con trol credit and the flow of money.

3. MARXISM

The world today finds itself beset by the scourges of communism and socialism, those twin doctrinaire off-spring of Karl Marx.

No corner of the globe has escaped the impact of these two dread political diseases, and the United States is no exception. The trend toward a socialist state is unmistakable as the Federal Government takes unto itself countless powers over the American people that give bureaucracy more and more control over them.

From without, we suffer from the threat of the world Communist conspiracy.

Our substance is drained in an effort to protect our own and other nations simply because this Administration is incapable of devising *political* weapons which might undermine, weaken and eventually neutralize the threat.

Its only solution is armaments and more armaments that siphon billions from the treasury and deplete the national wealth.

From within, one socialist scheme after another, all officially advocated, call for the Government to take money away from the American people in the form of taxes and hand it back to them encumbered by endless rules, regulations and restrictions.

As these are enacted either in whole or in compromise, they constitute a further drain on the substance of the American economy.

As the Government gains more and more control over the people, the American system of freedom and equal justice under the law recedes proportionately.

Slowly but surely the twin Marxist doctrines are turning the clock of civilization backward toward the Dark Ages of monarchical rule, and serfdom. *What is proclaimed to be liberal is in reality the blackest reaction and it should be spelled out as such.*

4. MORALITY

Long-time centralization of power in the hands of a few is a certain symptom of approaching moral decay. Brazen political philosophies of "something for nothing" become part of the electoral appeal. As government morals decay, so do the morals of those governed.

College basketball gambling scandals and dope-peddling rings on high school playgrounds are recognizable symptoms that the moral fabric of our people is in process of disintegration.

Not law, but a moral revival both in government leadership and in all walks of public life, is clearly called for.

5. TAXES

Combined Federal, state and local taxes have now reached the point where they are taking 31 percent of all national income. This is the highest level in American history and is only nine percentage points short of the 40 percent collected in socialist Britain which has brought that once great nation to the brink of ruin.

Taxes are the chief weapon of the socialist planners. The scheme is as simple as it is diabolical. In its most elemental terms it amounts to government performance of some function, formerly left to the citizen, by the means of imposing taxes upon him to finance the government's activity.

Thus, a citizen who formerly paid his own doctor bills would, under socialism, get medical services "free," but his taxes would be raised proportionately.

In other words, as the citizen becomes less and less self-supporting, he becomes more and more dependent on government simply because he has less and less left in his pocketbook after taxes.

Thus, the easiest way to lead a people into socialism is to tax them into it. *In truth, it is "taxation by misrepresentation."*

41

6. AGRICULTURE

The farmer has become resentful of what he increasingly suspects to be Government manipulation of farm prices for political reasons.

There is ample evidence that the Administration deliberately rigged the grain markets during the 1948 election campaign to force farm prices down in an effort to discredit the Republican 80th Congress.

In fact, under this Administration, the Department of Agriculture has been turned into a political agency to the detriment of the American farmer.

The present Secretary of Agriculture, with the President's backing, is openly advocating a farm plan which would deliver the farmer into a straightjacket of bureaucratic rules and impose a tremendous additional tax upon the public. Violations would be penalized by fines and jail sentences.

This Brannan plan calls for the farmer to sell his product in the open market at going prices and for the Government to then pay a subsidy to the farmer to make up the difference between the open market price and parity.

This is probably the most fraudulent scheme, against both farmer and consumer, that has ever been devised.

Its effect would be to drive down open market prices, keep true farm prices artificially high, while underwriting the whole phony business by heavy taxes against the consumer.

Even assuming that everything would work equitably, which it wouldn't, the American farmer would still become the prisoner of a bureaucratic government —*which is precisely what the Secretary of Agriculture seeks.*

7. DECENTRALIZATION

The high rate of centralization of power in Washington is slowly strangling state and local government to death.

Forty years ago, out of all government monies spent, the Federal Government expended twenty-six percent, state governments fourteen percent, and local governments sixty percent.

*Today out of all government monies spent, the Federal Government expends eighty percent, state governments, eleven percent, and local governments, nine percent.**

In Montgomery County, Ohio (Dayton**), for example, a Chamber of Commerce survey disclosed that the local government cost approximately $17,000,000 annually, while the Federal Government took out of Montgomery County in taxes approximately $200,-000,000 annually, *or almost twelve times as much.*

In 1951, the city of Dayton, in an attempt to raise money to build a new high school and a badly needed city building, had to submit a bond referendum to the voters. It was rejected.

Dayton's school teachers are underpaid, schools are terribly crowded and numerous other community

* These percentages are fairly accurate estimates.
** Dayton facts are approximate.

facilities are deteriorating rapidly simply because the county and city governments dare not impose additional burdens on the people while they bear the stupendous tax load which the Federal Government has fastened upon them.

What is happening in Dayton is happening in every community in America.

State and local fiscal problems are growing almost beyond solution without Federal aid.

The American people—who once had daily and watchful contacts with locally elected public servants responsible for tax expenditures—now find that government has become a cold, impersonal bureaucracy, *hundreds of miles removed from them and beyond their control, even through the ballot box.*

8. PEACE

Peace is the product of leadership. It is not a commodity which can be purchased. It is achieved only by working out an over-all, long-range strategy with fixed and resolute goals.

Those in power in Washington in these fateful last twenty years have had no such policy. They have wandered aimlessly in the field of international relations, improvising on the basis of expediency with neither ultimate goals nor an over-all strategy in mind.

The basic reason for the succession of disasters in international relations has been the failure of those in power to understand fully the nature of the forces loosed on the world.

44

Specifically, they have had little grasp of the true nature of the trend toward statism in the world. Sympathy for oppressed peoples caused them to move against Hitlerism, but they neither understood nor grasped its reason for being.

They have been even more blind to the origins of the worldwide communist conspiracy which many persons in the Administration regarded as nothing more than a mild extreme of liberalism.

Consequently, it is no mystery that they have failed in bringing peace to Europe as they destroyed Hitlerism, or that they have failed so utterly in combating communism.

They have operated, in their aimless fashion, on the premise that the will to resist communism can be gained by huge outlays of money—*that the dollar is a substitute for leadership.*

They have shown little or no initiative, imagination or ingenuity in the use of political weapons—*propaganda, counter-agitation and economic devices*—which many profound students of the communist conspiracy believe would be far more effective and far less expensive than the massing of armed might.

A whole new approach to the international crisis based on real leadership and real statesmanship is of the most vital need in America today.

The policies that produced the decisions at Teheran, Yalta and Potsdam, the decisions in China and Korea, have spelled out seven consecutive years of losses to the communist conspiracy. Not peace but war is the only likely outcome of such a course.

The political candidate and the political party who can spell this out best are going to make a profound impression upon the American people—*because they know deep in their hearts that something is fundamentally and basically wrong and the time for a change is at hand.*

SPECIAL NOTE

Before turning to the question of doing the things that win votes the problem of the Government employes' vote should be considered.

Government employes have been counted by pessimists as being in the bag for the party in power. At the present time, even the office workers in Government departments are ashamed to admit they work for the Government, because of the scandal surrounding the State and Treasury Departments in particular.

The candidate should make it a point to register with people on Government payrolls the fact that he wants the public to know that the great majority of them are loyal, hard-working and honest people, and that they should be proud once more to say they work for the United States Government, when he becomes President.

It is recommended that the candidate say nothing that would indicate wholesale firings of Government employes is in prospect. In the first place it would be a physical impossibility to fire them in any great numbers.

In the second place, most of them are disgruntled

and disgusted with Government operations as they see them and really want a change. It is suggested that a direct appeal be made to Government workers indicating to them that efficient, tireless and patriotic Government employes are civil servants and should enjoy the status of anyone who does his job well in any field of endeavor.

PART III

DOING THE THINGS THAT WIN VOTES

Both Republican candidates have warm and winning personalities. Both have a high degree of salesmanship in their manner. They are individuals who would normally be welcomed as visitors in almost one hundred percent of the living rooms of America.

Obviously the thing to do is to gain entrance for them into the homes of America by every means possible so that the warmth of their personalities can be felt. Here are some fundamental means of accomplishing this objective:

1. TELEVISION

TV offers the best, although most expensive, medium to carry the personalities of the candidates to the firesides of America. The traditional, major campaign speeches must be televised so that the public will completely comprehend the political philosophy which the candidates advocate. This is an absolute necessity.

But these "set" speeches, by their very nature, cannot impart the real warmth of personality with which both candidates are endowed.

Therefore, informal, intimate television productions addressed directly to the individual American and his family, their problems and their hopes, are necessary to make the most of the ticket's human assets. These productions should be made on film *with the best directional and technical facilities employed.*

2. PERSONAL APPEARANCES

In every campaign there arise numerous opportunities for a candidate who has a natural and instinctive love of people to quite naturally visit some home, shake some hand, write some person or a dozen other things which impart this love of people to the public-at-large better than any speech or campaign pamphlet.

These should not be stunts. They should be natural occurrences.

A keen judge of public relations of this sort should be assigned to each candidate for the sole purpose of being alert to such opportunities and the fullest exploitation of them.

3. LITERATURE

Campaign literature can be too slick, too voluminous or too dull. Pictures, particularly when the candidates have winning personalities, are worth volumes of words. It is recommended that the literature of this campaign be largely of the pictorial type, with the

selection of photographs being determined on the basis
of those that *best impart the warmth of the candidates'
personalities.*

4. PHONE CALLS

New phone-answering devices are available which
will enable us to stage a telephone drive in the last
ten days of this campaign that will be completely
unique in American politics.

The candidate in advance can make a number of
very brief tape recordings (thirty seconds and sixty
seconds in length). These would be in the nature of a
personal message from the candidate to the person on
the other end of the phone.

Phone answering equipment would be set up in all
key communities, both large and small, throughout
those states considered battleground in character.

Spot newspaper ads, radio and TV "spot" station-
break advertisements with campaign workers an-
nouncing the magic telephone number in each city
which could be dialed by anybody wanting to talk to
the candidate. Facilities for this type of operation are
available in all Bell Telephone offices, and phone-
answering equipment, while not inexpensive, is reasonably priced.

*The messages from the candidate would be sufficient
in number to enable him to put in a plug for individual
Senators and Congressmen seeking election in each
area, thus engendering their enthusiasm for him and
helping unite the whole campaign effort.*

49

This is a top secret project that would require an extensive amount of preliminary organization that should start immediately. *It cannot be set up at the last moment.*

5. MOTION PICTURES

Film productions made for television should also be distributed for 16 mm showings throughout the nation. Facilities for such distribution are now partially set up but a much broader, thoroughgoing plan must be devised.

6. CAMPAIGN PHOTOS

The nation should be plastered with pictures of the two candidates. Their so-called "campaign" photos should be chosen because of their quality for selling the warmth of the personalities. The usual "blow-ups" for rallies are indicated.

7. BILLBOARDS

The central selling stimuli of every billboard should be the campaign pictures of the two candidates, together with a warm, friendly slogan.

8. BUTTONS

Campaign buttons should be simple, possibly containing only two words—"I like." This type of button would be in keeping with the tone of warmth which this portion of the plan envisions.

In addition to these activities, every communications device of this modern age should be employed to insure full coverage of the entire electorate.

These include the following efforts:

RADIO

While TV is the most effective medium that can be used today, it needs to be supplemented by radio to reach 97,000,000 Americans, many of them living in remote areas impossible to reach except by radio.

RADIO & TV SPOTS

The use of radio and TV *station-breaks "spots"* during the last ten days of the campaign is a *must* for stimulating the voters to go to the polls and vote for the candidates.

SLIDE FILMS

Slide film programs have already proven very effective in politics. The Republican Congressional Committee was the innovator of the political slide film program. It was used on a trial basis in the 1950 campaign with outstanding success. Films for the 1952 campaign, dealing with specific political issues, are now available.

It is recommended that a national drive be launched to promote the use of the slide film technique. Consideration should also be given to the application of slide film technique to television in the production of television shows arguing specific political issues.

NEWSPAPER ADVERTISING

This medium is important but its use has been over-emphasized in past campaigns. It should enter this campaign at its point of relative value.

TRAVEL

The mode of travel of the candidate should include the airplane wherever possible, and when employed its use should be dramatized. For example, plane-to-ground telephone communications could be released to the press and radio. Escort planes could pick up the candidates' planes as they approach their destination, etc.

COORDINATION

It is imperative that the campaign be planned to show a united front among all national candidates—presidential, senatorial and congressional. Victory in all three fields is essential to a successful campaign.

Close team play between the candidates for the presidency and vice-presidency on the one hand and senatorial and congressional candidates on the other, is necessary to convince the public that the party is imbued with a winning spirit.

Fortunately TV and radio offer a unique and potent opportunity to demonstrate to the people that the national and local candidates are all working together in close harmony.

Here is how it can be done:

When the presidential nominee makes a major address on radio and TV, approximately two minutes at the opening and close of the program would be reserved for the support of candidates for the Senate and House in each station area.

Thus, is the speech originated from Chicago, it could be localized in Massachusetts, for example, by having Senator Lodge introduce the presidential candidate. With subsequent addresses Congressman Martin or the gubernatorial candidate could make the introduction.

Similar introductions would be made by local candidates in each TV or radio station area. These talks would be made in advance, on film for TV and recordings for radio, so that all would be identical in length, permitting all stations to cut back to Chicago or other city at the same time to pick up the nominee's address.

At the end of the presidential nominee's speech, the local announcers throughout the country could immediately cut in on the roar of applause, at a given signal, with an announcement requesting viewers and listeners to keep the program on for a few seconds more to receive a personal message from the presidential nominee.

These personal messages would also be made in advance on film or recordings and would be localized to each station.

Thus in Massachusetts again, the presidential candidate would urge the reelection of Senator Lodge,

Representative Martin and other congressional and state candidates by name. In Ohio this concluding talk would name Ohio's senatorial and congressional candidates—and so on round the nation.

This would be an innovation in politics and would generate a maximum of good will and winning spirit, all up and down the ticket, from top to bottom. It would help relieve senatorial and particularly congressional candidates of the enormous financial burden which they face if they attempt individual TV and radio campaigns.

By such close cooperation and coordination the total amount of funds spent in behalf of candidates, at all levels of operation, could be cut by substantial margins, and the money saved by integration of the national and local campaigns could be channeled into other operations such as the payment of workers on election day.

But most important of all, it would evidence to the voters that the Republican Party is united in a winning drive!

PART IV

WHERE AND WHEN TO SAY AND DO THEM

A national campaign is won by pinpointing a maximum effort in the right places at the right time. A keen sense of local conditions and acute instinct for timing are essential. It goes without saying that little effort should be wasted on Mississippi. It goes without saying that little is gained by addressing an agricultural speech to farmers during harvest time—they will be too busy and won't hear it.

In the 1952 campaign there are 25 states where the Republican effort will be crucial.

This figure is determined by the following reasoning:

A. *To capture the presidency,* 266 electoral votes are necessary.

B. *To capture the Senate,* 49 Senate seats are necessary for the barest majority. Of the 47 Republican seats now held, 21 * are in contest in 1952.

Of the 21 Republican Senate seats in contest, only 6 can be said to be "safely Republican." They are the contests in Maine, Vermont, North Dakota, California and Nebraska (two seats). The other 15 contests are in the states of Massachusetts, Connecticut, New York, New Jersey, Delaware, Pennsylvania, Ohio, Indiana, Wisconsin, Minnesota, Missouri, Utah, Nevada, Montana and Washington.

Of the 49 Democrat-held seats, only 14 are in contest in 1952, and of these, 5 are in the Deep South and are eliminated as a consequence. Three others are in the states of Rhode Island, Arizona and New Mexico where the Republicans have not won a single Senate seat in almost a quarter of a century, although

* This figure includes the California seat where the incumbent Senator won both nominations and, therefore, is not likely to face any serious opposition in November.

today there is a revitalization of the party occurring in Arizona and New Mexico under recently-elected Republican governors, and, of course, these states should not be overlooked.

The remaining six Democrat seats in contest are all in the "critical" categories as far as the Democrats are concerned. These six contests are in Connecticut, Maryland, West Virginia, Kentucky, Michigan and Wyoming.

Thus, if we add the 6 "critical" contests for Democrat-held seats to the 21 contests for Republican-held Senate seats, we discover that *the total of the 27 contests takes place in 25 states.*

C. *To capture the House,* where all 435 seats are in contest, it is necessary to win 218 seats. Of the 202 seats now held by Republicans, 4 of them have been gerrymandered out of existence by state legislatures in the past year, [and] therefore, the base figure becomes 198 Republican seats.

Of these 198 seats, 25 can be said to be in the "critical" category.

Of the 237 remaining House seats, 25 can be said to be "critical" for the Democrats and good prospects for the Republicans.

Thus, if we add the critical 25 Republican-held seats to the 25 Democrat-held seats in the same category, we get a total of 50 House contests that will determine whether the Democrats or the Republicans control the 83rd Congress.

Of these 50 critical House contests, 43 of them are in the 25 states where the 27 Senate contests occur.

314 ELECTORAL VOTES

California	32	Minnesota	11	Ohio	25
Connecticut	8	Missouri	13	Pennsylvania	32
Delaware	3	Montana	4	Utah	4
Indiana	13	Nebraska	6	Vermont	3
Kentucky	10	Nevada	3	Washington	9
Maine	5	New Jersey	16	West Virginia	8
Maryland	9	New York	45	Wisconsin	12
Massachusetts	16	North Dakota	4	Wyoming	3
Michigan	20				

D. Placing these 25 states in a "critical" category, we discover that they have a total of 314 electoral votes—48 more than the 266 necessary to elect a President. It should be noted that these 25 critical states do not include New Hampshire, Illinois, Kansas, Iowa, South Dakota, Colorado, Idaho and Oregon, all regarded as Republican states in most elections, with a total of 70 additional electoral votes.

Conclusion: These 25 critical states actually mean the difference between winning or losing a Republican President and a Republican Congress.

Therefore, it is recommended that these 25 states, with their 314 electoral votes, their 27 important Senate and 43 House contests, be the main focal points of the campaign together with special treatment which may be needed for Arizona, New Mexico and Illinois.

An additional reason for the recommended concentration in 25 states follows: In the 1948 campaign, organized labor and the left wing employed a new strategy concentrating their major efforts on Senate and House seats, leaving the fortunes of the Presidential ticket to ride the coattails of that effort.

The result of that strategy was astounding. The Republicans lost 9 Senate seats and control of the Senate, and 75 House seats and control of the House.

The Democrat candidates for the House amassed a plurality nationally of 2,800,000 votes, compared to President Truman's plurality of 2,200,000 votes. In other words, President Truman ran 600,000 behind the House Democrat candidates.

To look at the reverse side of the coin, Governor Dewey in the 1948 election carried 16 states, *but* of the 75 House seats lost in that election, 32 of them were lost in states that Dewey carried.

Candidates generally blamed this contradictory result on the fact that Governor Dewey disassociated himself from the record of the 80th Congress, thereby making it difficult for incumbent Republican members of that Congress to campaign effectively.

Thus, it can be seen that the combined labor, left wing strategy of concentration on Senate and House seats, and the Dewey strategy of disassociation from the Republican record in Congress, resulted in a disastrous defeat for the Republican party in a year when all experts of all political persuasion were unanimous in forecasting a certain Republican victory.

Therefore, *it is recommended* that the national campaign of 1952 be closely integrated with the Senate and House races for the maximum effect for everyone involved from the top of the ticket to the bottom.

The timing of the speeches is extremely important. Under present circumstances, particularly under conditions existing in the Midwest, it is recommended that a formal Acceptance Speech to the public be made around the approximate date of August 21.

This date is desirable lest adverse conditions in the Midwest begin to set like cement. It should be a hard-hitting, definitive address aimed at revealing the candidate as an aggressive man with both feet firmly on the ground, so far as issues are concerned. It should also contain appropriate references to the need for the two-party system and the desire of the candidate to strengthen the party. And, it should invite Democrat support as a means of bringing those presently in control of the Democratic party to their senses.

Under ordinary circumstances the recommendation would be to start the campaign about September 15, pacing it so that it would progress on a crescendo note to a terrific climax just before the election. But as indicated, we are not operating under ordinary circumstances.

Therefore, it is proposed that the Acceptance Speech on the approximate date of August 21 be followed by a three-to-four-week lull during which the candidate will make no major speeches, limiting his utterances to press statements, exchange of letters, telegrams, etc. The major portion of the campaign thus would be launched some time between the dates of September 15 and September 25.

It is recommended that the campaign be paced to carry out the candidate's promise to go into every nook and cranny of the nation in making his fight—with a barnstorming "whistle-stop" tour of the country by train and plane between the eight to ten major speeches.

The "where" for making the Acceptance Speech is very important. Because of the situation in the Midwest and the necessity to correct it at the earliest possible moment, *it is recommended* that the Acceptance Speech be made in Indianapolis, Indiana, which, of course, is at the midpoint in the Ohio, Indiana, Illinois area.

Tradition calls for a *"reason,"* usually a personal one, for the candidate's choice of the speech site. In the center of the Indianapolis business district stands Indiana's Soldiers and Sailors Monument on Indianapolis' famed Circle. The Circle has been the site of several memorable political speeches—FDR, for example, attracting a crowd of 50,000 there in 1932.

It is recommended that the Acceptance Speech be made from the steps of the Soldiers and Sailors Monument. It is suggested that 12:30 noon hour be chosen for the time.

As a *precaution* against bad weather there are a number of very large meeting places available in Indianapolis:

Cadle Tabernacle, only a few blocks away from the Circle (seating capacity approximately 12,000).

Butler Field House (seating capacity approximately 18,000).

Fair Grounds Coliseum (seating capacity approximately 12,000).

Fair Grounds Cow Barn (seating capacity approximately 10,000). The Cow Barn is adjacent to the Coliseum and frequently has been used for overflow crowds for political rallies held in the Coliseum.

Indianapolis has television and radio facilities, sufficient hotel accommodations and transportation, both air and rail, to meet any demands upon it contingent to an Acceptance Speech. All the major wire services have bureaus there.

It is recommended that state leaders, candidates and other party notables from adjacent states be urged particularly to attend the Indianapolis Acceptance Speech *for a maximum display of party harmony.*

The timing of the major campaign speeches and their locale should be kept flexible. A recommendation in July might prove worthless in September. However, at this moment it appears that the first campaign swing should, at least, be considered in outline form.

The "where" factor is also worthy of present consideration. The enormous growth of television introduces a brand new element. A television viewer loses all sense of "where." *He has the feeling that the candidate or performer is right in his living room.*

There are now 17,700,000 TV sets in America. Advertising agencies calculate an average of three viewers per set, or currently an audience of 53,000,000. This means that one-third of the population is now reachable by TV.

In addition, television sets are being purchased at

the rate of a half million per month. Thus by mid-October the number of sets will be in the vicinity of 19 million and the viewing audience will have grown to approximately 58 million persons.

Thus, for approximately 58 million persons, the locale of the candidate's speeches and appearances will assume relatively little importance. This fact produces two recommendations:

1. "Localization" of speech material in major utterances should be held to a minimum. A viewer in the Midwest or East is likely to turn off his TV set if the candidate deals at length with such subjects as reclamation, grazing rights and watershed development, even though this subject would have great appeal in the Rocky Mountain area.

2. In determining the locale of major speeches, the television factor relieves some of the pressure to have these speeches in cities like New York, Pittsburgh, Chicago and other areas served by TV.

It should be noted that *there is television coverage of the most populous areas of 20 of the 25 critical states* which have been selected for the focal point of the campaign.

Before we take up the recommended first campaign swing, it should be explained that there is another element that should be considered in addition to the TV factor. It is the tradition of campaign swings. In other words, local leaders expect certain things to be done because they have been done in the past. . . .

Governor Dewey started his campaign on September 20 traveling across Illinois and Iowa for whistle-stops with a major speech in Des Moines, Iowa, on the night of September 20. This swing covered Denver, Albuquerque, Phoenix, Los Angeles, Fresno, San Francisco, Seattle, Spokane, Missoula, Great Falls, Mont., Salt Lake City, Cheyenne and Jefferson City, Mo., the swing being completed on October 3.

The final Dewey swing commenced on October 26 with appearances in Chicago, Cleveland, Boston, North Attleboro and New York City.

Governor Warren's swing covered the period September 15 through October 16. It was a continuous trip covering Salt Lake City, Pueblo, Albuquerque, Tulsa, St. Louis, Louisville, Columbus, Detroit, Buffalo, Springfield, Mass., Hartford, Newark, New York City, Philadelphia, Baltimore, Pittsburgh, Charleston, W. Va., Chicago, Madison, St. Paul, Casper, Butte, Tacoma and Eugene, Oregon. It is to be noted that Warren's whistle-stops became very numerous after October 1, but that during the first fifteen days of the swing he made no whistle-stops at all.

The first campaign trip recommended is one through the Midwest, on the assumption that healing gestures will still be required there. This swing should start approximately September 20.

If it develops that harmony has been restored in Ohio and Indiana, between the delivery of the Acceptance Speech on the approximate date of August 21 and the start of this first campaign swing, the schedule might be revised.

In any event, Illinois should be included in the first

campaign tour because of the selection of its Governor as the Democratic presidential nominee.

The following areas are proposed for inclusion in the first trip with the belief that they may require additional attention on the final swing:

West Virginia, Ohio, Indiana, Illinois, Wisconsin, Missouri, Iowa, Nebraska and Minnesota.

The following major cities are suggested for coverage in the first swing with appropriate whistle-stops to be inserted as can be worked out with transportation experts and local leaders:

Monday, September 22	Milwaukee, Wisc.
Tuesday, September 23	Minneapolis-St. Paul, Minn.
Wednesday, September 24	Des Moines, Iowa
Thursday, September 25	Lincoln, Nebr.
Friday, September 26	Kansas City-St. Louis, Mo.
Weekend, September 27–28	Springfield, Ill.
Monday and Tuesday, September 29–30	Columbus, Ohio
Wednesday, October 1	Charleston, West Va.

This proposed swing offers the candidate a weekend in Springfield, Illinois, the home of Abraham Lincoln, giving him ample time to confer at length with state and local leaders in an area where the situation is critical.

By ending the trip in West Virginia, the candidate could take a few days of rest at White Sulphur Springs before starting the second swing which presumably would cover the Rocky Mountain States and the West Coast.

For the vice-presidential nominee it is proposed

64

that he concentrate his initial efforts in the Eastern States so that he can become widely known in that area at the earliest possible moment.

Suggested itinerary follows:

Tuesday, September 23	New Haven, Conn.
Wednesday, September 24	Boston, Mass.
Thursday, September 25	Springfield, Mass.
Friday, September 26	Syracuse, N. Y.
Weekend, September 27–28	Buffalo, N. Y.
Monday, September 29	Pittsburgh, Pa.
Tuesday, September 30	Reading, Pa.
Wednesday, October 1	Newark, N. J.
Thursday, October 2	Wilmington, Del.
Friday, October 3	Baltimore, Md.
Saturday, October 4	Hagerstown, Md.

It is also recommended that the presidential nominee attend the National Plowing Contest at Kasson, Minnesota—in Dodge County about 25 miles south of Rochester—which is being held September 5 and 6. It is understood that President Truman plans to attend this event as he did in 1948 and make a speech.

It is suggested that our presidential nominee attend on the second day, September 6, in an attempt to force the President to take the first day, September 5. Acting in deliberate contrast, he would make no formal speech but spend as much time as possible driving through the crowd, which may be as high as 100,000, shaking hands with as many as he can reach, possibly laying his hand to a plow, cocking his foot on a fence post and doing all the things he did naturally as a young man in Kansas. Any informal speech given should be brief, warmhearted and anecdotal or reminiscent of his youth and knowledge of farms.

It should be recalled that President Truman attended the National Plowing Contest in 1948 when it was held in Iowa and scored tremendously. It eventually proved doubly effective because of Dewey's failure to make the proper appeals to the farmer or to make a major farm speech.

The Maine election on September 8 should be given special attention if a field survey now being made indicates that we can come out of the state with a substantial victory.

Proceeding from the assumption that the survey will be favorable, it is suggested that the following efforts be made with a maximum of ballyhoo:

a. The National Chairman should visit Maine for a series of conferences.
b. Prominent out-of-state speakers should be scheduled for a series of consecutive nightly meetings in the state.
c. Assuming that the presidential nominee will have made an Acceptance Speech in August, it should be followed by an initial major speech by the vice-presidential nominee in Maine with a national radio hookup.

PART V

FUNCTIONS: WHO WILL SAY
AND WHO WILL DO

The functions of the campaign should be coordinated as closely as possible.

To do this, it is obvious that there must be one central clearing house for all operations. The obvious instrument for this function is the Republican National Committee Headquarters under the direction of the Republican National Chairman.

The following organizational chart has been designed to bring about a *maximum of coordination and cooperation* between the Republican National Committee, Republican Senatorial Committee, Republican Congressional Committee and the Eisenhower-for-President Clubs.

[Here "Document X" contains a chart showing how the campaign should be organized.]

You will note that the two candidates and their staffs have *direct liaison* with the Chairman.

The Chairmen of the Republican Senatorial and Congressional Committees are brought into the operation in a direct advisory capacity so that the functions which they perform can be closely integrated into the campaign effort—*and still maintain the legal separation which is required under existing Federal statutes.*

A similar status is given the Eisenhower-for-President Clubs under the heading *"National Volunteers for Ike."*

67

Two new groups are recommended: (A) *The Strategy Board;* (B) *The Advisory Committee.*

The First—the Board of Strategy—is composed of the Republican National Chairman, the Republican Senatorial Chairman, the Republican Congressional Chairman and the Republican National Chairman's three assistants—the Executive Director, the Organizational Director and the Publicity Director.

It is recommended that this Advisory Committee act as an Intelligence Agency, or a field G-2. It should be chosen from among the most astute political judges the party possesses in each of the various categories. Thus a state treasurer in one state would be responsible for semi-weekly reports to the National Chairman, the governor of another state could be engaged in an identical role, a national committeeman in another state, etc., etc.

One of the great weaknesses in past campaigns has been the inability of the National Chairman—or Campaign Manager—to obtain true field reports from on-the-ground experts—such as this proposed Advisory Committee will provide. An attempt to cure this by conference phone calls provided a distinct improvement in 1948, and it is believed that the Advisory Committee technique will be a further improvement.

It is recommended that all major utterances, important press releases and other material which might reach the public from the candidates, or spokesmen for them, be cleared at all times with either the Chairman of the National Committee or one of his assistants.

Conversely, public moves by the Chairman or any of his spokesmen should be imparted to the candidates if they are of sufficient importance to require their attention.

The closest liaison in this respect is highly desirable.

PART VI

RECAPITULATION

To summarize, this campaign plan calls for the following main objectives:

1. *A forceful, hard-hitting attack by the two nominees made in such a fashion that it will appeal to the vast numbers of the 45,000,000 Stay-At-Homes.*

2. *A sales approach in television, radio, personal appearances, literature, photos and other campaign material that will best capitalize on the warmth of personality of both nominees.*

3. *A coordination of TV and radio time between the national nominees on one hand, and the senatorial and congressional nominees on the other, so that the latter may obtain prominent broadcasting time at the most effective hours of the day with only a modest outlay of money in their particular districts.*

4. *Concentration of the campaign in 25 critical states:*

Maine	*New Jersey*
Vermont	*Pennsylvania*
Massachusetts	*Delaware*
Connecticut	*Maryland*
New York	*West Virginia*

Kentucky	*Nebraska*
Ohio	*Missouri*
California	*Utah*
Indiana	*Nevada*
Michigan	*Wyoming*
Wisconsin	*Montana*
Minnesota	*Washington*
North Dakota	

In these critical states, 27 Senate seats, 43 House seats and 314 electoral votes can be won. In addition, special treatment is recommended for the states of New Mexico, Arizona and Illinois.

5. An Acceptance Speech in mid-August followed by a hard-driving campaign with the rate of acceleration calculated to reach a terrific climax just before the election.

6. A closely integrated campaign organization bringing into harmonious relationship all national elements of the party to achieve a united drive.

CONCLUSION

A political campaign based on these recommendations will avoid the mistakes of the past.

It will make the maximum use of existing facilities and introduce innovations that should inspire Republican workers, disaffected Democrats, Independents, Stay-At-Homes and Young Voters to work with a zeal that should spread like a prairie fire.

The stirring spectacle of the Republican party at

long last in high gear, employing aggressive methods and generating militant spirit in every segment of the party, will do more to convince the American voters that their deliverance is at hand than any other single thing that we can do!

If we have the courage to face unflinchingly the problems outlined in this plan and the proposals for their solution, and above all else, to make the decisions NOW which will give this campaign the powerful directional force which it needs, we will score a landslide victory on November 4!

III

THE NIXON CRISIS

In Humphreys' files is a small batch of notes, scribbled in pencil:

> Art—
> tell him
> to intercept
> Dick before
> he says something
> to *press*
>
> Ike's phone number
> Superior
> 1-6979
> Dick should
> hold at
> that airport
> until you
> have talked
> to Ike

He
Must
intercept
Nixon

They're
crappin'
you—
not left
yet

—Main 1—
1504—
opened up
between you
and Dick at
airport while
you get Ike
out of bed—

Tell Dick's
guys to open
the wire

The date was September 24, 1952. The time: A bit past 6 A.M. Dressed in pajamas, Humphreys was sitting in a room in the Carter Hotel in Cleveland. Sitting beside him, also dressed in pajamas, was Art Summerfield. They were making calls to Republican leaders all over the U. S., to Nixon and his aides in Los Angeles, to Eisenhower's aides, to Senator Robert A. Taft and others. Sometimes, it was Summerfield who made the calls. Sometimes, it was Humphreys. While Summerfield was on the phone, Humphreys kept passing him notes, telling him what to say. He must have been in a state of high excitement. Normally, Humphreys wrote in a small, tight hand. He wrote these notes in a huge scrawl.

If Humphreys was, in fact, excited, the reason is easy to understand. The whole future of the Eisenhower campaign was at stake. For days, Humphreys had fought desperately to keep Eisenhower from dumping Nixon. Now, he was fighting just as desperately to keep Nixon from quitting as Ike's running mate. Nixon was ready to quit. As Stewart Alsop has remarked, Nixon is part Irish, and the Irish in him is explosive. He usually manages to keep himself under control, but sometimes he can't. He showed that when he appeared on television right after his defeat by Pat Brown in his race for Governor of California in 1962 in a display of disappointment and rage that shocked the nation. This time, he was just as mad. Only his closest aides—and Humphreys, who told Summerfield, knew it—but he was ready to say: "To Hell with it. I'm through."

Humphreys had known Nixon since he was a freshman Congressman. He liked and respected Nixon. However, even if Humphreys had detested Nixon, he still would have worked to keep Ike from repudiating him, and to keep Nixon from resigning as Ike's running mate. To Humphreys, it was a simple matter of practical politics: Eisenhower and Nixon had to stick together because, if they split, in the ensuing chaos Adlai Stevenson would be certain to win.

With the help of Summerfield and others (including Taft), Humphreys did succeed in keeping Ike from dumping Nixon, and, in those four, frantic hours on the morning of September 24, 1952, he did succeed in bringing Nixon back into line. Had he failed in either attempt, the whole future of American politics would perhaps have been different. Humphreys almost certainly was right: Ike would have lost the election. Ike, himself, thought so; he told Sherman Adams so. Nixon never would have been Vice-President. He never would have been able to run for President in 1960. He never would have been able to run again in 1968. In those four hours in the Carter Hotel, Humphreys actually made it possible for Nixon to become President of the U. S. sixteen years later.

Part of this story has been told before. It began on September 8, 1952, when the New York Post *ran an interview with Dana Smith, a California attorney, in which Smith admitted the existence of a "secret Nixon fund." Actually, there was nothing secret about the fund. In the final analysis, whether or not one considered it reprehensible depended almost entirely on whether one was a Republican or a Democrat. However, Eisenhower had been running as "Mr. Clean." On the very same morning the* Post *story appeared, the New York* Herald Tribune *had proclaimed: "HONEST DEAL IN U. S. PLEDGED BY EISENHOWER," while the Washington* Daily News *had bannered: "IKE SAYS WHAT WE WANT NOW IS 'THE HONEST DEAL.' " Under the circumstances, the* Post *story actually created consternation in the Eisenhower camp, and not merely among the amateurs like William E. Robinson, then publisher of the now defunct New York*

76

Herald Tribune *and General Lucius Clay, who had recommended Nixon to Ike. Many of the professional Republican politicians panicked, too. Sherman Adams was a cold, New Hampshire granite face: He did not demand that Eisenhower dump Nixon but neither did he call on Ike to embrace Nixon. He just asked questions.*

Humphreys didn't hesitate a moment. From the first he knew it was essential to victory that Eisenhower keep Nixon and that Nixon stay with Ike. He fought the men around Ike down the line on this. It was he who suggested that Nixon appear on TV to explain the fund, who demanded this and who arranged for Nixon's TV appearance.

The result was "the Checkers speech." A critical failure and a political success. Television writers called it a soap opera, but it saved Nixon's political career. Paradoxically, it also was the reason Nixon blew up and started talking about resigning as Eisenhower's running mate. Shortly before Nixon went on the air, Thomas E. Dewey had called him to say that a survey by Herbert Brownell showed that a majority of the Republican leaders wanted him to resign. When Nixon got off the air, he expected Ike to issue a statement applauding him. Instead, all Ike did was say that he wanted to meet with Nixon at the earliest possible opportunity. After Dewey's call, Nixon, understandably, was near the breaking point. Ike's bland statement was the last straw.

Murray Chotiner, Nixon's political strategist, phoned Humphreys and told him that Nixon was talk-

*ing of chucking the campaign. Humphreys grabbed
Summerfield. That's how the phone calls started that
morning of September 24, 1952.*

*There are in Humphreys' files two memoranda to
Sherman Adams telling how it happened. The first is
dated February 7, 1959. It begins:*

Concerning the Nixon episode in 1952—

Frank Kluckholn, formerly of *The New York Times,*
working for me in the '52 campaign, walked into my
office midmorning Thursday, September 18, 1952, and
left a piece of wire copy on my desk urging me to read
it. I was so busy at the time that I could not pick it up
for so much as a glance. Sometime during the noon
hour he phoned to see if I had read the copy. I was out
of the office in some kind of a huddle. About 2:30 he
came at me again. I read the piece. It was a UP account of the New York *Post*'s so-called exposé of the
Nixon fund. . . .

Looking at the wire copy, it was evident to me that
the Democrats were going to do everything possible to
blow up a big storm.

I telephoned upstairs (from the second to the fourth
floor of the Washington Hotel) to the Nixon headquarters to discover when they would be talking to the
Nixon train again (the practice was for someone to
open a telephone wire into Washington off the Nixon
train or plane at every stop to keep posted on things).
I was told that the train was due to stop somewhere in
Oregon in thirty minutes, so I said I wanted to talk to
Nixon. I quickly dictated a statement in which Senator Karl Mundt charged "a left-wing smear" and de-

lineated some of the ultra-radical escapades of the New York *Post* and its editor, and we released it. I then rushed upstairs to get on the phone with Nixon. Instead, I talked to Chotiner who said the stop was too brief for Nixon to get on the phone. I asked him if they knew about the *Post* story and he replied they did and that Nixon had met with the newspapermen before they rolled into the stop and had told them that it was true he had a fund—nothing more. Apparently they were taking it rather casually. I told Murray I thought the thing was going to be much bigger than we dreamed, read him the Mundt statement and strongly urged that Nixon go on offensive with the same angle. (This, Nixon did, commencing at the next stop.)

I went back downstairs to my office and set up a call to Art Summerfield on the Eisenhower train as soon as it reached Des Moines. When I got Art half an hour or so later I filled him in on everything and strongly urged that nothing be said from the train that was *not* in support of Nixon. I said we had to put up a solid front. Arthur agreed completely and I think you will recall that that was his position throughout the episode. . . .

Meantime, in Washington, I was attempting to check sentiment around the country. Frankly, and I so reported to Arthur in Kansas City, the Nixon story hadn't even made a small dent on the public consciousness, and next to none on the politicians. The public generally was not paying a bit of attention. The real furore was, in my opinion, confined to the Washington and New York press corps, the Eisenhower train, the Nixon train, a few top-level party leaders and friends of Ike's, and a few editorial writers who called for Nixon's resignation. But what one hell of a furore it was in those circles.

I was also during the day promoting statements in behalf of Nixon and I well recall that when I phoned Bob Taft in Cincinnati he told me that he already had issued a statement on behalf of Nixon on his own motion an hour earlier and that "I think the whole thing is ridiculous."

Meantime, also on Friday, the Democrat and left-wing rumor factories were cranking up. I was getting phone calls about all kinds of ludicrous things Dick was supposed to have done with the money, much hinting that huge sums of cash were being passed around, etc., etc., and I understand that you people on the (Eisenhower) train were getting them also, because by Saturday I became the focal point for passing these rumors on to Nixon and this operation continued from Saturday right up until Tuesday evening when Nixon made his famous broadcast. This is the way it worked: The rumors would be passed on to me from the train, or elsewhere, and I would phone them to Chotiner. One pip of a rumor I will relate later which you will probably remember.

Incidentally, over Saturday and Sunday there developed in the party leadership ranks a strong suspicion that there was sentiment on the train to dump Nixon. This was increasing the frequency of phone calls from responsible political leaders into headquarters.

On Saturday morning I got up with the idea that we ought to put Nixon on TV in as dramatic a way as possible, following a pet theory of mine that when adversity hits, try to convert it into something you can capitalize on.

I thought about it for an hour or so and then telephoned Art in Kansas City. While he was favorably impressed, he raised the very pertinent question: "Where do we get the money? We simply haven't got it." I replied that maybe we could get Nixon on a sustaining program and promised to look into it. But I told Art I thought it was more important, with so much at stake, that our decision to put Nixon on TV, whether paid or free, should be considered by the best brains in the party. I had made up a list of people I had proposed to consult during the day and Arthur took them down on the phone. I know I had eight or ten names and that they included Taft, Martin, Tom Coleman, Halleck, etc., Roy Roberts of the Kansas City *Star* and others. About a half hour later either you telephoned me and said you wanted the name of Bill Robinson, of the New York *Herald Tribune*, added to my list, or Arthur phoned me and told me your wishes.

I spent all day Saturday phoning leaders around the country discussing the proposal to put Nixon on TV. The reaction was unanimous by 7 o'clock Saturday night to do it. But I still had one phone call to complete, despite the fact that I had tried the call repeatedly all day. It was to Bill Robinson. I didn't get him until approximately 9 P.M. and I discovered that I was talking to him through the *Herald Tribune* switchboard connected to the locker room of a golf club. The reason I hadn't been able to get him was he

81

had been playing golf all day. I explained the entire proposal. His reaction was something like this: "Bob, I wouldn't put him on TV; I'd throw him off the ticket."

It was the only adverse reaction I got. The Eisenhower train had moved to St. Louis during the day for Ike's speech to the convention of the Federation of Republican Women's Clubs. I phoned the findings to Art Summerfield—in other words, approximately ten to one in favor of putting Nixon on TV. Art still was troubled by money and wanted me to explore the possibility of free time.

I stayed up most of Saturday night–Sunday morning trying to find some, but my heart wasn't in it because I felt that we had to control the timing; furthermore, that nobody was going to give us the time and, if they did, they would have to give the Democrats equal time. . . .

Sometime midmorning Sunday, Art telephoned me from St. Louis and told me to get on the next plane and get out to St. Louis. He said he wanted me to talk with the General and that this had been agreed to. I recall that I had a deuce of a time finding a plane on which I could get a seat but that I finally got on a puddle jumper run by TWA through West Virginia, Ohio and Kentucky towns. It was running late and I could only get clearance to Louisville.

When we arrived in Louisville I refused to get off the plane. Several TWA people spoke nicely to me, but I wouldn't budge. Finally, they took off with me aboard, but this caused another half-hour delay and it seems to me I did not get into St. Louis until 5:30.

Art was at the airport to meet me but, as you recall, it is another hour into St. Louis from the airport, so we didn't get to the hotel until about 6:30. Art then discovered that the General had left for a dinner party at somebody's home in St. Louis and that we were going to meet with you in your drawing room on the train.

Arthur was not feeling very well, but the two of us headed immediately for the station and met with you in the drawing room, he and I on one side of the table by the train windows, and you on the other.

Most of the discussion which, it seems to me, lasted about a half hour or more, was conducted by you and me. Arthur was saying very little because he was half ill.

To put it in the fewest words, you and I had it hot and heavy. I was proposing several ways for the whole controversy to be handled and you were most caustic in your reaction to each of them. In addition, I was putting forth every argument I could think of that Nixon must be kept on the ticket. You didn't think much of my arguments and said so. (You didn't argue that he should be bounced either—it was simply a matter of non-acceptance of what I was saying.)

I recall that you were particularly incensed when, at one point—probably in my complete disgust at what I regarded as an unnecessary controversy that was only helping the Democrats—I asked you: "What do you plan to do, change every piece of literature, every billboard, every campaign poster, every sticker in the land with Nixon's name or picture, and how the hell do you think we are going to do that?" Your

83

reply was icy almost to the point of absolute zero centigrade.

I remember I had to sit a full minute to get hold of myself because I had broken through the boiling point.

Finally, I said to you: "All right, answer this one: On Friday morning in Nebraska the General said, 'I intend to talk with him at the earliest time we can reach each other by telephone.' Do you mean to tell me we can convince the American people that for the last sixty hours Dick and Ike have not been able to get together on the telephone when anyone knows that all the General has to do is pick up the phone and call him. No wonder everybody thinks there is a plot to throw Nixon off the ticket."

[Here is where my respect for Adams took its first great leap in our short acquaintance.]

Instead of jumping across the table and throttling me, you, without any comment whatsoever, turned and picked up one of the phones and gave instructions that a phone call be set up from the General to Nixon to be completed when the General returned from dinner.

Having finally accomplished something, I turned to Arthur and said: "Let's get out of here." Which we did.

As you know, the famous phone call was completed that night, the General and Nixon talked for the first time since the whole storm blew up. I assume that the decision to buy television time was reached at that point or as a result of the conversation, because at about eleven that night Arthur was notified that we were going to buy the time and we worked all night from our suite in the Jefferson Hotel trying to find the money and getting the thing set up.

(Incidentally, I have never known with whom the General had dinner that Sunday night, but I was told at the time that the opinions expressed around the dinner table to him were unanimous that Nixon should be thrown off the ticket.)

As we worked all night I recall that Len pledged $25,000 of the $75,000 it would take to put Nixon on TV, and then having committed this sum from the Congressional Committee funds and discovering that we couldn't locate Everett Dirksen anywhere, Len then "pledged" a like amount from the Senatorial Committee funds in Everett's behalf. (This didn't set very well with Ev later and we were a couple of weeks getting the adjustments made, but it was finally paid.)

By 8 o'clock next morning we were on the track, with the money raised and the time agreed to and ordered. The Eisenhower train had pulled out of St. Louis at 4 A.M. but sometime Monday morning we got the word from the train that I was to get on a plane and go to Los Angeles to help produce the Nixon show. I strongly advised against it, arguing that Nixon should be completely on his own, that nobody should tell him what to do and I contended that we would get a better result if he did it that way. I did this for two reasons: (1) it appealed to me that Nixon must be in a position of having no outside counsel if the public was to be convinced that here was a man telling his own story in his own way and (2) that Nixon was far better at this type of thing than any of us, including BBD&O, Kudner and the whole kit and kaboodle of advertising and public relations experts in our retinue.

But Arthur was insistent. So I flatly refused to go. For this piece of insubordination the next pressure was for Arthur himself to go to Los Angeles. By 3 o'clock that afternoon I had convinced him that this would be even worse than if I went. By approximately 4 o'clock we got on a plane and went back to Washington and I believe by that time there had been general agreement established that everybody would let Nixon alone.

This does not mean that we were not in communication with the Nixon camp, because we were. In the 24 hours preceding the broadcast I must have talked with Murray Chotiner a dozen times, but the subject was confined to passing on to Chotiner the various questions, rumors and angles that were being raised by newspapermen, columnists, Democrats, Republicans and what-have-you. I know this much: Chotiner did not know what Nixon was going to do at any time because he told me so during our conversations and this was only developed incidentally because I deliberately wasn't raising the question.

Some time shortly after noon Tuesday, the day the broadcast was to be made, Arthur discovered that Bill Robinson had joined the train at Cincinnati that morning and was with Ike whistle-stopping across Ohio to Cleveland that night where the General was to make a major speech on tariff. On the basis of that development Art said he and I were going to hop on a plane to Cleveland. I argued that I could be of little value, for him to go ahead by himself.

About an hour later he phoned me from the Washington airport and told me he was holding the plane until I got on it. I went out the door without even my hat and Arthur and I flew into Cleveland arriving at the hotel just as the Ike parade ended and the General entered to go to his room.

We got a suite and about twenty minutes later Jerry Persons came around to our room. Then he and Arthur went around to the General's suite.

About ten minutes later I got a call to come down to the General's suite.

When I got there I found Stephens, Cutler, Seaton and others sitting around the living room and I was ushered across it to a long narrow room where there were twin beds. You were just inside the door and at the other end of the room sat Arthur and Jerry Persons. The General was half reclining on a twin bed facing them.

You remained standing somewhere near the door on the other side of the room throughout the following—

Jerry said approximately the following:

"Bob, you've been very helpful checking out the various rumors about the Nixon finances, but we have one here that seems to have a fairly good source and we wondered if you could check it fast for us. We have been told that the Nixons redecorated their house and retained a Georgetown decorator to do it for $10,000. When the work was completed, Mrs. Nixon paid the entire amount in cash."

I said: "I don't have to check it. I know the answer.

"I was over at the Nixons' a week ago Sunday night and Pat was in the living room with Dick when I arrived. We began exchanging pleasantries and I said to her, 'That is a stunning circular couch, where did you get it, Sloane's?' She answered: 'We brought it from Whittier—it was in our house there.'

"I said: 'Those beautiful drapes—don't tell me they didn't come from Sloane's?' Pat answered: 'No, the material came from Lansburgh's and I made the drapes myself.'

"We talked about one or two other pieces of furniture and then she went upstairs to put the children to bed and Dick and I went about our business.

"There is absolutely no question in my mind that this rumor is wholly false."

My recollection is that Jerry and Arthur agreed verbally. Beyond saying hello to me when I came in the room and something when I left a minute later, I don't recall the General having a single comment one way or the other during this incident. Nor do I recall your saying anything.

After dinner Arthur and I returned to the General's suite and, as I recall it, about twenty people lined the room including all those already mentioned, plus Senator Carlson, Bill Robinson, Hagerty—in fact, virtually everybody who was on the train attached to the General's party.

When Art and I entered it was perfectly obvious

that the General was sampling opinion around the room on what to do about Nixon. I recall Frank Carlson was talking as we entered and, while I do not remember him taking any firm position, he seemed to be arguing for Nixon, because Bill Robinson kept interrupting him making points that suggested Nixon should be off the ticket.

Next, at the General's invitation, Bill had his say which was definitely anti-Nixon.

Then the General said: "What do you think, Sherm?"

You had your chair tilted against the wall (I think) and you brought it down to the floor. It seemed to me that you took nearly a full minute before you replied.

I don't recall any of your words except I got the definite impression you were avoiding taking a position.

Then the General asked Art for his views. Art went all out for Nixon and argued that the General should be prepared to say that he was all for Nixon after the broadcast.

There was one incident while Arthur talked. Art said something that obviously made Ike mad. I remember distinctly that the General's opening words of his one sentence were said with a glare on his face and he was biting off the words obviously in anger, but by the time he ended the sentence he was all smiles and conciliatory in tone. This self-control—displayed clear across the spectrum of human feelings in the space of one sentence—impressed me deeply, so much so I don't remember a damned word he said, nor the subject that irritated him.

Bobby Cutler was next. If I recall correctly, and I think I do, he was the one who advanced the idea that there had to be a face-to-face meeting between the General and Nixon before the thing could be completely settled, regardless of what the broadcast produced. I recall nobody particularly agreeing with this, in fact I am sure Arthur probably vocally opposed it, but after all, it was what finally happened.

About this time somebody issued a warning that we all had to go to the hall where Ike was to make his speech, before which he would watch the broadcast. We all piled out of the hotel into cars in the motorcade to Convention Hall . . .

In setting up arrangements with the Convention Hall manager, I had another bright idea. Governor McKeldin was to be on our ABC-TV network that night. I telephoned him in Annapolis and asked him if he would agree to be in the Baltimore studio on a "standby" basis telling him that it just might happen that we would want to give the McKeldin time to Ike after the Nixon broadcast. He readily agreed.

Then I phoned BBD&O and told them to alert ABC that we might want to shift the point of origination and gave them *several* cities from where we might want to do this, so they could not spot the fact that I included Cleveland.

Next, I phoned the ABC station manager in Cleveland and asked him to string up a telephone wire and a microphone from the station to Convention Hall and make a tape recording of Ike's speech, telling him that I would pay the charges. I also made

90

certain that I would be able to locate him at an appropriate time before the 10:45 broadcast, if needed.

When we got to Convention Hall you will recall that we all climbed endless stairs until we arrived at the manager's suite of offices at the crow's-nest level.

The offices consisted of three large rooms opening into each other and we had the first one which was approximately 20 by 25 feet. In one corner the manager had placed a TV set, angled out into the room. About fifteen feet away, along the left wall from the TV set, he had placed a sofa for Mr. and Mrs. Eisenhower at right angles to the wall.

Altogether there were approximately thirty people in the Convention Hall manager's office while the General watched the Nixon broadcast there. Most of these people were off the train, and, of course, there were several local bigwigs present. I recall we had quite a commotion when a local news photographer managed to break through and take a picture of the setup, but he was finally allowed to take shots and leave just before the broadcast.

The General sat at one end of the couch next to the wall, Mrs. Eisenhower occupying the other end which reached into the middle of the room. Bill Robinson sat next to her on a straight chair, the back of which was against my desk.

(I'll not try to impose my memories of the next thirty minutes on you—you undoubtedly have your own.)

At the end of the broadcast the most enthusiastic

91

Nixon supporter in the room was Bill Robinson. In thirty minutes he had done a complete about-face.

There was a quick huddle in the center of the room where the General decided he would abandon his speech.

Somebody must have ushered most of the people out of the room because about five minutes after ten the General sat down at a long table against the wall on which the TV set was placed. In that position he wrote his own remarks on the Nixon telecast in longhand, with a din ringing in his ears from the hall downstairs where the audience was stamping its feet in rhythm to the chant: "We want Nixon."

I recall no one consulting with the General, nor he with anyone, about what he intended to write. Approximately six or seven minutes later he rose from the table and he, Persons, Art, Hagerty, and I (were you there?—I can't be sure) went into an adjacent office and closed the door. There he read out loud to us what he had written. I pointed out that there was no communication to Nixon as yet and the General quickly dictated a telegram to Nixon which Jim Hagerty took down in longhand and this became part of his remarks. Everybody then rushed downstairs and the General started speaking. Only I stayed behind.

I had the phones already opened into National Committee Headquarters and I recall that when I got back on the phone at this moment the chief operator came on the line and told me I had better keep it open if we intended to keep in touch with the National

Committee Headquarters "because we are simply swamped with telephone calls—every light on this board is lit up; I've never seen anything like it."

. . . Just to refresh your memory, not only was the National Committee switchboard swamped for the next 24 hours, but more than 160,000 telegrams were delivered to the National Committee (Western Union had to import operators to Washington to handle the traffic, they were five days getting them delivered, and they were weighing them instead of counting them.) In addition, we received over 200,-000 pieces of mail which took us a month to open using nearly one hundred volunteers. In this mail were $62,000 in contributions, one being $1000, one for one hundred dollars, and the balance being made up in literally thousands of letters which contained anything from a quarter to ten dollars. The Washington Hotel made more than half of its lobby available for this mail-opening operation because we had run out of space in the hotel.

There were 18 million TV sets in the country at the time and Nielsen reported that 9 million of them were turned to the Nixon show. This is three times the biggest Nielsen rating General Eisenhower had during the campaign and nearly four times bigger than any Stevenson had, and to the best of my knowledge is still, to this day, by far the biggest political audience in TV history . . .

I think the General ended his speech at approximately 10:35. This gave me ten minutes in which to put the General's remarks via tape on the ABC network at 10:45 in place of McKeldin. A phone call to New York and a phone call to the local station manager took care of that.

As soon as the General had concluded his remarks, Persons, Mundt and Les Arends—all traveling with the General—and Arthur came back upstairs and entered the manager's office. I had a telephone line open to Murray Chotiner and was talking to him.

What Murray was saying to me was so hot that I finally asked him to hold the phone a minute. I turned to Arthur, Jerry, Les and Karl and said:

"We've got plenty of trouble in Los Angeles that only you, Arthur, can straighten out. If you other three gentlemen won't mind, I think that when Arthur is through on the phone he will not be able to discuss it."

Jerry, Les and Karl all quickly agreed and Arthur commenced talking to Chotiner. The burden of the conversation was that Nixon might take himself off the ticket. He evidently did not feel that General Eisenhower's remarks were cordial enough.

The conversation had to terminate because the Nixon party was leaving for the airport to go to Missoula, Montana, to resume Nixon's interrupted campaign schedule.

After an interval of twenty or thirty minutes I again opened a telephone line to Chotiner, by then at the airport, and Arthur tried to get Nixon to the phone. Chotiner said Nixon was on the plane and wouldn't get off of it.

We said we would call Nixon in Missoula.

Clutching this secret to our breasts, Arthur and I

went back to the hotel suite sometime in the middle of the night (the Ike Special pulled out of Cleveland for West Virginia at 2:00 A.M.) and tried to get an hour of sleep before we talked to Nixon. We had decided that we would try to promote a Wheeling, W. Va. meeting that night if we could get Nixon back in the frame of mind to stay on the ticket.

We got together with Dick at 6:00 A.M. Cleveland time. First Arthur would talk to him and then I would talk to him. Sometime during this twenty or thirty minutes on the telephone, I discovered that Cleveland newspapermen were huddled against the outside door eavesdropping. While I was running them and the photographers down the hall—mind you, this was 6 A.M.—Arthur evidently got Dick somewhat mollified, because when we got back in the room he finished the conversation and our job was twofold:

1. To get a commitment from the General that Nixon was staying on the ticket before Dick would even consider going anywhere to meet the General.

2. Finding out (a) how we could get in touch with the General, by that time rolling across southern Ohio; (b) would the Wheeling airport be big enough for Dick's DC6 to land there; and (c) if so, could we get an agreement out in time so that the plane could make the trip from Missoula to Wheeling for a reunion that evening.

By numerous phone calls back and forth we discovered that Arthur probably could talk to the General when the train stopped at Portsmouth, Ohio, at 9 A.M. Believe it or not, we had a hell of a time finding out if a DC6 could get into the Wheeling airport, but we finally discovered it could. Then we began operations to have Dick's plane ready to make the flight from Missoula to Wheeling. . . .

Although Humphreys does not mention this in his memorandum to Adams, probably because Adams already knew it, Summerfield did obtain a commitment from Mr. Eisenhower to keep Dick Nixon as his running mate. He then called Chotiner in Missoula with the news. Only then did Mr. Nixon agree to fly to Wheeling.

Humphreys' memo to Adams concludes:

At the next Ike Special stop—Ironton, Ohio— Arthur talked to you on the phone and told you everything was set—that Nixon would arrive in Wheeling at 9:30 that night. As you know, the Eisenhower speech was delayed until after that hour to accommodate the reunion.

You can believe it or not, but neither Arthur nor I were off the phone from 6 A.M. until 10 A.M., and we went into this entire stretch in our pajamas with no breakfast.

Somewhere during the night, or possibly Wednesday morning, after talking to the General in Portsmouth, Arthur ordered a telephone poll of the National Committee members, and from Wheeling that night the General read a telegram from Arthur saying that of the 107 members of the Committee who were reachable out of a total membership of 138, the 107 were unanimous in support of Nixon.

When Mr. Nixon's plane landed in Wheeling, Mr. Eisenhower was in the waiting crowd. He darted up the ladder and said: "Where's the boss of this outfit?" A correspondent answered, "Up there, General." Mr. Nixon was helping Mrs. Nixon with her coat. "What are you doing here, General?" he asked. "You didn't have to come here to meet us." Mr. Eisenhower put his arm around Mr. Nixon and said: "I certainly did, Dick. You're my boy."

Later, Mr. Eisenhower announced that Mr. Nixon had "completely vindicated himself." Mr. Nixon said: "This is probably the greatest moment of my life."

IV

TECHNIQUES OF POLITICAL PROPAGANDA

From the moment he joined the Republican Congressional Committee as public relations director, Humphreys' basic strategy was: Attack. In 1949, with the Democrats in control of both houses of Congress as well as the White House, there was, of course, no alternative. However, even after Dwight D. Eisenhower swept into the Presidency in 1952, this remained his basic strategy. In a memorandum to Len Hall, prepared in 1953 for submission to President Eisenhower, he told why:

. . . One final thought is that . . . it would be a political mistake for this Administration to rely solely on its achievements. These achievements must be judged against the performances of the predecessor Administration. Political warfare must be waged by selling our philosophy, our achievements, our kind of government against the alternative.

The Democrats campaigned not only on their

achievements but also against the picture of an opposition which had brought on a depression and would bring on another because it placed profits ahead of people.

We do not want to build up any false pictures. But we will have to do unpleasant things in taxes, in budgets, in defense and in foreign policy because we face a hostile force in the world. The strength and power of that force was built up substantially because those in charge misjudged the situation. They were soft to communism. They are still soft. They are reluctant to admit past mistakes. This disables them from facing the threat as it is. One of the great issues in the country is an honest fear for national survival if our destiny is returned to the hands of those who are flabby in appraising and dealing with the communist menace. The people are entitled to judge us and to judge the opposition as to our ability to appraise that menace and as to our firmness in dealing with it.

Therefore, it is clear, and it is axiomatic in politics, that we must publicize the faulty judgment and lax action of the opposition as well as our own record of achievement . . .

In another memorandum to Hall, entitled "Political Public Relations," also written in 1953, Humphreys reiterated his philosophy:

Politics is the presentation of a choice to the people.

If Political Party A speaks only of its affirmative actions and does not undertake to characterize the alternatives offered by Political Party B, then it is doing only half of its job. As in all forms of conflict, attack is the strongest political weapon. It is axiomatic in politics that you must have an enemy.

The Republican Party has always been weak on the attack. It has tended to be too "statesmanlike." Its record of conducting investigations, which are a form of attack, has not been as good as that of the Democrat party.

The party in power has an enormous advantage over the party out of power. It has the "biggest megaphone in the world" in the White House; nothing else compares with it.

In their effectiveness in the conduct of public relations, the dissemination of information, the launching of attack and the promulgation of party line, the following ratings can be applied:

1. The President.
2. The White House.
3. The Vice-President.
4. The Attorney General, the Secretary of Agriculture, the Secretary of Defense, and the balance of the Cabinet in that order.
5. The Senate leadership.
6. The House leadership.
7. The National Chairman.
8. The Sub-Cabinet members.
9. The National Committee.
10. The balance of the Senate.
11. The balance of the House membership.
12. The Senate Campaign Committee.
13. The House Campaign Committee.

The chief complaint heard throughout the nation both from plain citizens and party workers is either (a) "The Eisenhower Administration hasn't done anything," or (b) "The Eisenhower Administration isn't selling what it has done." There is a close relationship between these two standard complaints.

Here is a frank analysis of what causes the complaints:

    a. The Administration hasn't picked an enemy.

    b. It hasn't spelled out its program—one, two, three, four, etc.

    c. Attempts by lesser echelons to pick the enemy and to package the program have not been successful because it is like employing a piccolo to do the work of a full orchestra. (See above effectiveness ratings.)

    d. Cabinet and Sub-Cabinet members have been too engrossed in the mechanics of their own operations.

    e. Senate and House members have tended to steer individual courses because of lack of party line.

The following recommendations will go far toward changing the entire public relations picture:

    I. The obvious enemy is "the Marxist left wing," both socialist and communist hues. The Democrat party, because its leadership is from the left wing, need never be attacked except in that connotation.

II. The one-two-three program containing an extensive political "it" for submission to the next Congress would provide the missing package.

III. Maximum use of the biggest "megaphones"— the President, the Vice-President, the Cabinet, etc.

IV. Elimination of public relations men at all levels who do not know their business.

V. Better liaison between all of the "megaphones."

VI. Complete exposure by all means possible of all ramifications of the twenty-year drift to the left, plus exposure of their current activities, including deliberate promotion of an economic depression.

On Point IV, Humphreys badgered Hall. In a memo entitled "Publicity and Party Line," he wrote:

. . . One thing which would make our selling effort more powerful would be to eliminate the hold-over publicity men [in government agencies] from the Administration. Over half of the top men charged with selling the achievements of their agencies were, less than a year ago, selling the achievements of those who want us to fail.

Selling the achievements of any Administration involves a lot more than explaining and popularizing its record and its achievements. That's an important part, but the way in which something is accomplished, its timing, the manner of announcement are just as important. That is primarily in the hands of agency public relations men and we don't dare talk politically to some of them . . .

103

Still another memorandum to Hall, this one entitled "Political Salesmanship" and dated December 7, 1954:

1. MEDIA

The job of selling the point of view of a political party varies according to whether the party is in power or out of power. When a political party is in power it possesses the greatest megaphone in the world—the White House. And that is where the spearhead selling must be done. When a party is out of power it uses its next biggest megaphone, its members of the Senate and House.

The role of the National Committee at best is a supplemental and advisory agency. Its function is to see to it that the necessary *ideas* are generated for the megaphones, be they the White House when in power, or the Senate and House members when out of power. A National Chairman and a National Committee are a mere whisper compared to the product of the White House or the Congress.

2. SALES METHODS

There are three basic ways to political salesmanship: (a) attack, (b) affirm and compare and (c) repetition. It is the first of these, attack, that makes the front pages and the radio and TV networks. It is the second of these, affirm and compare, that tells the voter that he is getting a better product than he used to get. It is the third of these, repetition, which closes the sale.

104

3. PARTY LINE

A political party, to be successful, must have a "party line" to strengthen the supporting chorus to the big megaphones. "Party line" is only another way of saying "follow the leader." The party in power, possessing as it does the White House, has no difficulty laying down the party line if the White House lays it down clearly enough and often enough. On the other hand, the party out of power has some difficulty in establishing party line because of the diversity of its leadership. In the latter case party line almost invariably develops its attacks on the White House, simply because the minority party must cut down the effectiveness of the White House leadership if the minority party is to win. For this reason, it is imperative for the party in power . . . to sell its affirmative attack and comparison, lest it find itself in the fatal position of being wholly on the defensive.

4. MECHANISM

An instrument as politically huge as the Federal Government needs over-all guidance, not only from the management standpoint but the public relations standpoint. Under present operations it has the former but lacks the latter. The Office of the Press Secretary can scarcely be expected to handle its extensive and time-consuming duties and the tremendous over-all public relations management at the same time. A public relations counsel, concerned only with generating ideas and public relations policy, but not with execution, is needed. Such a public relations counsel not only must have mastery of his craft but have thorough experience as well. If created, the "Office of Public Relations Counsel" could provide the directional fiber in political salesmanship now so badly needed. It is recommended that the direction of public relations for the Executive Branch be located in the same place as the over-all management—the White House.

President Eisenhower took no action on Humphrey's recommendation for the appointment of a man to direct over-all public relations for his Administration. However, the recommendation was not forgotten. On taking office, President Nixon appointed Herbert Klein to fulfill precisely that job.

Humphreys naturally was concerned not only with strategy but also with tactics and techniques. An example of his thinking on propaganda tactics was a memorandum he wrote to Gerald D. Morgan, a White House aide. President Eisenhower was considering a message to Congress proposing a National Commission to rationalize the nation's tax structure. In what is probably a model guide on how to launch a legislative proposal, Humphreys wrote:

To achieve the maximum results [the] Presidential message [should] strike a few simple phrases that would enable the man in the street to identify himself and his future weal with the undertaking. Such phrases as "it is time to relieve the people of paying

106

taxes on taxes," and "a man pays enough taxes without paying four different taxes on a gallon of gasoline," etc. etc.

Assuming that an excellent message is drafted I would like to suggest the following organization of the publicity on it and subsequent implementation of the message:

1. There should be some buildup prior to sending the message to Congress. This might be done by leaking a story to *The New York Times* or some other newspaper on the eve of a press conference. In response to questions the President could then tell his press conference the next day that he was sending such a message to Congress.

2. Assuming the press conference to be held on Thursday, the message could go to Congress the following Monday morning with the White House press secretary advising the newspaper men of it for Monday morning papers.

3. An organized effort should be made by the White House to get the publishers of "bell-cow" papers, some of the more thoughtful columnists, some of the leading magazines and radio-TV commentators informed in advance and asked to have editorials and other supporting matter ready to follow immediately the delivery of the message. Examples: *The New York Times*, New York *Herald Tribune*, Philadelphia *Bulletin*, Baltimore *Sun*, Scripps-Howard papers, Knight papers, Denver *Post*, Los Angeles *Times*, Raymond Moley, George Sokolsky, Ray Tucker, David Law-

rence, *Newsweek, Time, Life, Look, Saturday Evening Post, Colliers, Pathfinder, U. S. News,* Earl Godwin, Ed Murrow, Fulton Lewis, Jr., *Three Star Extra,* etc., etc.

4. On Monday after the message is read, Senator Taft and Majority Leader Halleck should immediately announce they will introduce the bill the next day.

5. The bills should be introduced on Tuesday with accompanying press releases from Taft and Halleck.

6. On Wednesday, fifteen or twenty Republican Senators (Democrats not excluded if they want to do it) should ask Taft's permission to add their names as coauthors. (This is not feasible in the House where coauthorship is not possible under the rules.)

7. I think radio and TV time should be secured for Senator Taft to make a preliminary argument to the public for the proposition; this should be followed a few days later by a similar setup for Halleck.

8. The same attention paid publishers, columnists and so forth under Point 3 should be given the following:

  A. All Republican Governors and . . . many Democrat Governors urging them to immediately issue statements or release telegrams to the President and to the press endorsing the proposition, pledging their cooperation.
  B. The same tactics should be pursued with leading mayors across the country.
  C. Members of the Senate and House. . . .

D. National organizations as well as local [groups] should be contacted to lend their *public* support. Examples: tax foundations and taxpayers' leagues, Association of Mayors, municipal leagues, Governors' Conference, National Chamber of Commerce, state chambers [of commerce], National Association of Manufacturers, municipal workers unions and any other unions that could be persuaded to join the movement, women's organizations, school and teachers' organizations.

9. Leading citizens should be urged to give public support. Examples: Herbert Hoover, Bernard Baruch, various college presidents and so forth.

10. Experts in the field—such men as Harley Lutz, etc.—should be urged to do likewise.

11. The leading magazines such as *Saturday Evening Post, Colliers, Cosmopolitan, American Magazine, New York Times Magazine, Readers Digest,* etc., etc. should be contacted at editorial level and offered assistance and facts for articles about the problem.

12. The appropriate committees of Congress to which the resolutions would be referred should take a day or two of preliminary public testimony each and on separate days, on the ground that they want to be sure the resolutions cover enough territory.

13. Consideration should be given to the possibility of each state government, each municipal government and each county government naming a three man advisory committee to help the National Commission gather facts. These advisory commissions

might be very helpful but assuming they produced little, the mere appointment of them would make major news in each state and community.

14. From time to time the President himself should receive individuals or groups to discuss the problem and they should be authorized to make statements on the White House steps as they leave.

15. It goes without saying that the Commission itself should be set up in such a fashion that it would have adequate funds, facilities and personnel to keep the public relations campaign going after the preliminary campaign outlined above.

16. The heads of the major TV and radio networks and their program directors should be contacted to promote as much attention as possible to the proposition over the air waves . . .

I think the White House would do well to acquire the services of an expert publicist who would be assigned solely to this job and possibly later take a job with the Commission. I strongly advise against anyone of the three national political committees having any direct part in the venture.

On the question of propaganda techniques, Humphreys wrote innumerable memoranda. One, to John S. Wold, publicity director of the Wyoming Republican State Committee, dated April 19, 1958, on the subject of billboard advertising, shows how closely he studied the efficacy of the various media. Anyone running for any public office would do well to consider his observations.

Humphreys wrote:

110

I am happy to pass on to you the experience of others, the National Committee and myself, on poster-type advertising and I want to begin by congratulating you on making the inquiry. Several years ago I happened to work in a special congressional election and I discovered that the very day a bright young man was appointed campaign director he had bought $4,000 worth of billboards for an election that was going to be held thirty days later. Next, I discovered that the entire public relations budget was $5,000. So you will get some idea how useless this type of thing can be unless employed correctly.

I would like to make the following suggestions.

1. Billboard advertising is not cheap, yet in certain types of campaigns it is very effective, in others it is a waste of money. The best single thing that can be done on a billboard is to sell a name—and that is about all you can sell. The reason is simple, a billboard catches your peripheral vision. People gain impressions from them without even realizing they have seen them. It is almost subliminal in character. Even when they are on the bend of a road and you are driving straight at them, this largely holds true. Therefore, the ideal number of words on a billboard is six! At the most, ten (here, too, I know a wealthy finance chairman in the Midwest who not only put up the money for a very extensive billboard campaign but insisted on writing the posters. To have read them, a person would have had to park his car and sit there a few minutes, so the money was almost a total waste).

2. Billboard locations are very important. If you want the best ones you have to make reservations

111

months in advance. *It does not cost you anything to make reservations because there is a thirty-day cancellation clause.* Therefore, your committee could do no wrong in reserving its billboards now for September and October. Then you do not have to decide until July or August whether you want them or not. You will get much better location this way and you can actively seek them with a chance of getting them.

3. 24-sheets are the paper that is pasted on billboards and you have to pay for this. It is not cheap so you [had] better get the figures in front of your committee from a reputable poster outfit.

4. Candidates love to have their pictures on billboards and posters, but I have always pointed out to them that their pictures are not on the ballots and voting machines—it is their name that counts. The biggest thing on the billboard should be the name that you are peddling—not the picture unless the candidate is so attractive that it will really add value. People simply do not have time to look at a name and picture both when traveling thirty to sixty miles per hour, yet you may recall that our official National Committee billboard in 1952 consisted of the President grinning on the left and the Vice-President grinning on the right. Over the top of the pictures were the words "Ike and Dick." Between the pictures in large letters in different colors were the words "They're for You." At first glance, it did not have much appeal to some politicians, but after all, isn't that what most people want to know before they vote?

5. Message: If possible, a message should be sold with the name. For example:

112

Elect
George GUDE Governor
for *Good* Government
Vote Republican   Nov. 4

However, I have never felt that slogans are too important—it is the name that counts.

6. The when and why of using billboards to me is rather simple. If you have a brand new candidate whose name needs to be sold I would say that billboards are a must and the campaign to sell the name should commence very early and continue until election day. If the candidate and name are long established in the public mind it is possible to do without billboards completely or a minimum representative number simply to let the public know the candidate is still around. To give you an example, if Thomas E. Dewey were running for Governor of New York again this year I question whether billboards would even be needed except for a token showing. However, if Len Hall were the nominee I would say billboards were very important as Len's penetration is rather stratified at this point.

Here are some thoughts on fence and pole posters, sign cards, window cards, etc.—

1. I would say that everything I have listed above concerning billboards applies equally to posters, although I am not certain that Point 2 regarding reservations applies here. I don't know the setup in your state and you will have to check it. I just want to stress

113

once more that the name is more important than pictures on posters.

2. In many ways I think posters are as good, if not better, than billboards. Marcantonio, the late Communist-loving Congressman from New York, always used them extensively in stacks of three—in other words, he never put up a single poster. He would put up three posters, one above the other, and if a fence area was 20 feet wide he would put them three deep clear across the fence. It was most effective. You also might write George Christopher, the mayor of San Francisco, and see if he can give you information on the posters he used when he successfully ran for mayor in 1955. They were in weird solid colors (as I recall it, a strange green and a strange yellow with the color schemes reversed so that actually he would have two different posters). These could be seen at great distances and when headlights hit them they seemed to be luminescent. I have never seen them used anywhere else but they were terrific, and my recollection is they were stacked three deep also with the top and bottom in one color combination and the middle in the reversed color scheme. I want to stress that when you looked at them at three or four feet distance they repelled you because of the weird colors, but they were tremendously impressive at a distance and they were mostly posted in empty lots and fields so they were several yards away from the highway. All they had on them were the words "Christopher for Mayor," his name and the office for which he was running.

3. I think anything I have said about posters also

applies to streetcar, bus, and window cards, but of course you would have to use those singly.

I think I can best sum up by telling you a story: In late November or early December of 1949, I landed at the Chicago airport and drove to the Hilton Hotel. As we left the airport and started down a feeder road to the main highway I saw a huge billboard, advertising Everett Dirksen (no picture, just his name). When we got on the highway and started through the Chicago environs, every vacant wall, fence and many poles had posters with his name on them. The area was literally plastered with the name Dirksen. At that time Dirksen was the leading candidate for the GOP senatorial nomination in 1950 and it was assumed that he would win it, although the Democrats were supposed to win the election. But his weakness was that, while he was known fairly well down-state, particularly in the congressional district he had once represented, he was very little known in Chicago and Cook County; therefore, he had started one year early peddling his name in that area—nothing else. When I got back to Washington I told Len Hall here (the Chairman of the Congressional Campaign Committee) that while the politicians might not think Dirksen had too good a chance in November 1950, I would bet on him on the basis of what I had just seen. I still regard it as one of the smartest uses of posters and billboards I have ever seen, well worth whatever it cost. Today, with the Dirksen name established the length and breadth of Illinois, as a result of having served since his election in 1950, I would say such a billboard and poster campaign would be a waste of money because the name has been sold. If you stick to this formula, you can't go far wrong on billboards and posters . . .

Another memorandum on techniques of propaganda, this one written in January 1955:

Any educational program today must take into account the so-called audiovisual field—television, radio, motion pictures, slide films and tape recordings. NEA [the National Education Association] estimates that 90 percent of all educational facilities in the United States have either motion picture or slide film projectors, or both. Although accurate figures are not available, it is known that a sizable number of these facilities also have television, radio and tape equipment.

In addition, there are the great commercial television and radio networks which deal with the general public and have a certain amount of penetration in our schools. The television industry is expanding at a tremendous rate. In the last two years, for example, the number of television stations has almost quadrupled (approximately 120 at the end of 1953, compared to 450 at the end of 1954). Television, still in its infancy, has not begun to realize its educational role. For example, there is nothing comparable to the music education program conducted by the radio industry in the mid-1930's, notably under the leadership of Walter Damrosch. The field offers unlimited horizons.

Because motion picture film is more and more being used on television (instead of live performances), motion picture techniques become doubly important. The reason: Prints of suitable motion pictures made for television can be given additional 16mm distribution through educational facilities (TV also uses 16mm). Since the largest cost in the preparation of a motion picture film is the item of production, with print costs a negligible factor, the effective circulation of a motion picture on a viewer-cost basis can be greatly reduced. In addition, because of the growing use of motion picture film, costs are rapidly coming down and techniques enjoying a corresponding gain.

Thus it is possible to produce the same motion picture for both television audiences *and* schools.

Television programming for most stations is still a major headache and will continue to be so. There simply is not enough entertainment material to go around, nor enough sources producing it on quality basis. It is entirely possible that well-produced educational films could be sold to TV station program directors at a modest fee that would cover print cost and a proportionate share of production costs. This type of film would readily lend itself to local sponsorship by banks and other civic-minded institutions, thus making the product financially attractive to local stations.

Slide films have gained great acceptance in both the business and eductional worlds, not only because they are highly effective when well produced, but they are relatively inexpensive to produce. Our armed services discovered in World War II that teaching time could be cut in half by the use of slide films. For example, President Eisenhower, based on his World War

II experience, is a very enthusiastic supporter of slide film technique. Reason: Two senses rather than one are at work—both the eye and ear. Moreover, experience has shown that it is much easier to hold an audience or class with the slide film technique than with the usual lecture or teaching methods.

Tape recordings (or phonograph records), while not as attractive as the motion or slide film, nevertheless, because of vastly improved techniques, offer an inexpensive medium for the distribution of educational material . . .

In conclusion, it is reasonable to state that the whole audiovisual field has only begun to be explored from an educational standpoint. It offers a big area for a pioneering venture.

And, just in case anyone thinks Humphreys did not recognize the limitations of TV, here is a memorandum he prepared for the Republican National Committee on October 15, 1959. Entitled, "A New Approach to Radio-TV Usage for the 1960 Presidential Campaign," it reads:

In 1952 the Republican National, Senatorial, House and Citizens Committees spent approximately two million dollars on radio-TV presentations, three-fourths of that sum being expended for appearances by the presidential and vice-presidential candidates. In 1956 slightly more was expended, with approximately three-fifths of it going to personal appearances of the candidates for President and Vice-President, the balance for 4½-minute shorts.

I think the 1952 campaign was moderately successful for four reasons: (a) television was a novelty; (b) because of one-channel monopolies in most areas, people had to look at political broadcasts or nothing; (c) there was an intense interest in the outcome of the election; and (d) General Eisenhower was a great war hero.

I think the 1956 campaign was less successful for two reasons: (a) the novelty had worn off TV and virtually all channels had lost their monopoly status; and (b) too much reliance was placed on the 4½-minute shows, a useful format that was ineffective because of poor production by both parties.

It is obvious that neither political party has yet discovered the most effective use of national TV-radio time. The political package offered so far has a very low entertainment value, and entertainment is the principal thing being sought by people on TV. In addition, I think both parties have imposed on the patience of average TV-radio listeners by giving static performances, by poor imagery, by words which cannot be understood, by sentences which lack TV-radio clarity, and by the glaring failure to provide much, if any, showmanship.

A fresh approach to TV-radio usage is strongly indicated.

An election, particularly a presidential contest, is a serious business. A new TV-radio format should take this fact into consideration, but not become awe-stricken by it. For example: I see no reason why we should not apply the singing commercial and the animated cartoon techniques to our national campaigns.

119

I see no reason why people should not start whistling a catchy, hand-clapping GOP theme song.

In the two presidential campaigns in which we have experience, I think it can be stated without contradiction that the most successful TV-radio appearances by the candidates have been on question and answer shows, particularly the unrehearsed kind which the Vice-President had in Ithaca in 1956. TV-radio surveys show that speeches have a very low rating compared with the other fare on the air. The reason is simple: too long, too dull.

What should be done about TV-radio in 1960?

Two proposals follow:

1. The emphasis should be shifted from formal speeches (holding their number to a reasonable minimum) to the interview-type show, and the bulk of the TV-radio budget should be expended on commercial spots of less than one minute, employing animation and musical techniques where desirable.

2. The budget for TV-radio should be increased fifty percent (to three million dollars) and roughly two-thirds of this sum should be budgeted for spots of less than one minute, starting twenty days before election and reaching saturation intensity the final week, employing both TV and radio media.

I am convinced that we get more real results from each dollar spent by spending *more* money, contradictory as that may seem. I do not think a spot campaign such as we attempted in 1952 produced much for the dollar because of lack of repetition and lack of saturation.

Finally, I think we ought to do some pretesting in

the design of most of our TV material. We shoot from the hip. We have no knowledge of how good or bad we are going to be. We operate on production schedules so tight as to stifle creative thought and to preclude pretesting.

Therefore, I would like to make this additional proposal: That we commence now, in 1959, actually making animated cartoons, developing some singing commercials, experimenting with various types of interview techniques. This will cost money now, but I think it will save money once the campaign gets underway in 1960 because we will know where we are going.

V

TV WILL NEVER REPLACE
THE PRECINCT CAPTAIN

After the congressional elections of 1954, the Republican National Committee directed Humphreys to make a study of what went wrong. He had public opinion pollsters question voters in ten critical states, analyzed reports from state chairmen and defeated candidates, sent survey teams into New York, Pennsylvania, Illinois, Michigan, Minnesota, Oregon and Wyoming. He concluded that, while the Republicans had made blunders in strategy and tactics and even in the candidates they offered the voters, the basic reason for the Democratic victories was the efficiency of the AFL-CIO campaign organization, which had, in effect, become the Democratic campaign organization. Compared with the AFL-CIO, he said, the Republican organization was a shambles.

Humphreys' study of the 1954 campaign convinced him the Republicans never would become the majority party until they managed to separate labor's rank-and-file from its leaders.

On the question of labor's role in the campaign, he wrote:

In terms of cause and effect, the big Democrat turnout was the *effect;* labor's role was the *cause.* Unquestionably the most important factor revealed by the 1954 congressional elections was the startling display of strength by labor organizations, particularly those with leftish leadership. This was demonstrated most decisively in Michigan, Illinois and Pennsylvania and to a lesser, even though amazing extent, in Oregon and Wisconsin. Furthermore, there was scarcely a state where organized labor's effectiveness was not felt to a significant degree. To best understand labor's impact, it is necessary to examine what happened in Michigan in considerable detail.

MICHIGAN—THE "PILOT" OPERATION

The plain truth is that the CIO *is* the Democrat party in Michigan—they are one and the same thing. There is every evidence that the combined CIO-AFL forces enjoy almost the same strength in Illinois, Wisconsin and Pennsylvania.

Michigan, of course, is and has been, the "pilot" operation. Labor, in the 1954 Michigan campaign, finally arrived as the dominant force in the state.

The CIO, and to a lesser degree the AFL, is in politics 24 hours a day, 7 days a week and 365 days a year, year in and year out in Michigan. It has become as big a "business" for the unions as labor-

124

management relations. The amount of money available for this purpose is staggering, particularly when compared with the size of the coffers of the regular Democrat or Republican organizations.

All one has to do to understand how Michigan has been changed from a relatively rock-ribbed Republican state into a Democrat state in a period of less than ten years is to examine the CIO effort.

RADIO-TV PROPAGANDA

The UAW-CIO spends $125,000 a year in Michigan on radio and television "newscasts." There are two daily radio programs carried on CKLW, a 50,000 watt station, the first being a half hour in length, 6:15 A.M. to 6:45 A.M. to catch the working man as he drives to work, and there is a second program on the same station of fifteen minutes' duration, from 7:15 P.M. to 7:30 P.M., to catch people after their evening meal. This is Monday through Friday, 52 weeks a year. There is a television show over Detroit's biggest television station, WJBK, once a week. The TV station claims an audience market of six million, or approximately six-sevenths of the total population of the state. In addition, because the radio programs do not reach the Grand Rapids market, although covering the rest of the state, there is a fifteen minute daily program from the Grand Rapids station. Twenty-four other radio stations have CIO broadcasts at least once a week, some of them daily, and, of course, none of this includes the national CIO daily newscast called "John W. Vandercook and the News," which goes to many Michigan stations. The commentator or "newscaster" for all the state CIO shows, both radio and TV, is a gentleman named Guy Munn. His interpretation of the news and his observations of events amount to a continuous campaign of ridicule of industry, business generally, the Republican party and its candidates. Democrat Congressmen and the Governor appear frequently on the programs.

NEWSPAPER PROPAGANDA

One printer in Detroit alone published seventeen different CIO local tabloid newspapers, with a total weekly press run of 200,000. Seven others are published in other shops with a press run of an additional 100,000. The UAW-CIO publishes a monthly tabloid newspaper which is mailed to its entire membership throughout the country. The press run is 1,300,000 and in October this was increased to four million for purposes of influencing the election. Instead of the usual four pages, the publication in October was increased to eight pages and special "election editions" were run for the following: Wayne County, Michigan, Illinois, Iowa, Indiana-Kentucky, New York, Massachusetts, Delaware-Maryland, Ohio, Pennsylvania, California, Oklahoma, Connecticut, Tennessee and Minnesota. The press cost of this special edition alone was estimated at $56,000, and this figure does not include mailing, distribution and preparation costs, which undoubtedly are twice this figure, or an approximate total of $175,000. These special election editions were nothing more than out-and-out political endorsement tabloids, with pictures and biographies of candidates and headline endorsements. Out of the entire nation only two Republicans were endorsed; all of the others were Democrats. (The two GOP candidates were both in Pittsburgh.) A study of these publications, the 24 weekly publications or the monthly tabloid or the special election editions, discloses an incessant barrage of anti-business, anti-Republican, pro-Democrat slant for page after page. This propaganda attack is never-ending. It goes on the year around.

CAMPAIGN CONTRIBUTIONS

It is almost impossible to estimate the size of the campaign contributions from organized labor to Democrat candidates. It literally runs into the hundreds of thousands of dollars but very little of it is reported, and a great deal of it is very difficult to trace. For example, not a few Democrat candidates actually used CIO headquarters as their campaign headquarters, CIO headquarters staff as their staff, etc. An examination of the records of the Clerk of the United States House of Representatives and of some reported contributions in Michigan filed with the state officials shows that union after union contributed to Democrat candidates and were their chief source of campaign financial support.

127

ORGANIZATION

Under the personal direction of Walter Reuther, President of the CIO, a complete precinct operation was set up in Detroit and many other cities in Michigan. The organization plan called for each precinct to have ten workers under a "division" chairman. Over the division chairmen were "congressional district" chairmen. It is known that more than 500 persons were placed on the CIO payroll for campaign organizational work starting more than a month before the election and that they were paid twenty dollars a day each (a Republican or Democrat precinct worker is lucky if he gets thanked and sometimes they get five or ten dollars on election day.) There is no absolute proof of this pay scale except that it comes from extremely reliable sources and a story was printed about it in the November 7 issue of the Detroit *Times* and it was not disputed by anyone. Twenty dollars a day to ring doorbells during the campaign and to work at the polls on election day is an expenditure of money that can scarcely be matched by an ordinary political party. This news story commenting on the all-out effort by the CIO calls it a "dress rehearsal for 1956" and concluded, "Now that the dress rehearsal is over, the organization will aim at once toward 1956 when Lieutenant-Governor-elect Philip A. Hart will be running for Governor and [Mennan (Soapy)] Williams will be in the national picture in one capacity or another" (meaning President or Vice-President). Since election day CIO and AFL leaders in Michigan stated publicly that they have already started raising funds, shaping strategy and developing techniques for 1956.

RESULTS

Obviously, such a stupendous radio-TV and news-paper propaganda campaign, such an outpouring of funds and such a highly disciplined and financed organizational effort should produce results. And it did. Startling results! Governor Williams was reelected by a plurality of 250,000, or nearly 200,000 greater plurality than he had in three previous elections. Senator Homer Ferguson was defeated by a Democrat and two Republican Congressmen went down. *But most significant:* For the first time since 1936 the Republicans lost the entire state ticket. The Republicans even had their majority in the Michigan House of Representatives cut to the bone and the Democrats made gains in the state Senate. Michigan can no longer be counted as a Republican state.

OREGON THE SECOND EXAMPLE

Although labor's effort in no other state matches its efforts or dominant control in Michigan, it is nevertheless a fact that labor was responsible for the Democrat landslides in Illinois and Pennsylvania and loss of a Senator and Congressman in Oregon. In Oregon, labor's effort was concentrated in Multnomah County (Portland). Multnomah County's operation is selected for a brief analysis here because its pattern was followed, many times multiplied, in Illinois and Pennsylvania and other states.

129

Oregon had not had a Democrat Senator since 1914. It has been staunchly Republican and generally conservative throughout its history. Starting with World War II, the rise of labor unions and the influx of industrial workers caused Democrat registration to rise but this was not reflected at the polls in any great measure against the GOP in succeeding years. Richard Neuberger, a young magazine writer, found himself in 1954 with the necessity to make peace with Dave Beck's powerful Teamster's Union, which has the greatest membership of any union in Oregon. Neuberger had been hired by the railroads to write in their publications in favor of restriction on trucks and had, from a political standpoint, written unwisely. Early in 1954 (when he became the Democratic candidate for Senator) a meeting with Beck resulted in Beck's acquiescence to Teamster support of Neuberger. As a result, every labor publication in Multnomah County trumpeted in behalf of Neuberger throughout 1954 and at the same time launched a vigorous attack on Senator Guy Gordon, the Republican incumbent. The Portland unions first set up a "United Register and Vote Committee" composed of 24 of the state's top labor chiefs, representing every important union. These union groups performed two indispensable services for Neuberger: (1) They raised a tremendous amount of money for him and were instrumental in channeling money from the East into his campaign coffers. (2) They performed propaganda and organizational functions for the Democrat candidate. Unions which are notoriously unenthusiastic about

130

opening up their membership rosters gladly turned them over to the UR&V Committee.

The union membership rosters were broken down into single pages of ten names each and union wives made a quarter million phone calls during the registration and voting period, producing 13,000 new voters on the registration rolls. In addition, they mailed 98,000 letters to union members, urging them to vote for Neuberger.

On the two Saturdays preceding [the] election, special "flying squads" hit the street with each squad assigned to a concentrated neighborhood of workers' homes. Tens of thousands of pieces of literature and hundreds of signs, all paid for by the unions, were distributed by the flying squads. On election day the union wives got on the phone to make a follow-up call to every person previously telephoned. Democrat precinct poll watchers and election board members were largely union members.

When a tally was taken of the 6:00 A.M. to 6:00 P.M. vote on election day, Gordon appeared in excellent shape. However, the polls are purposely kept open in Portland from 6:00 P.M. to 8:00 P.M. and, as labor had planned, these were the hours in which union members voted by the thousands. Result: Neuberger carried Multnomah County by 16,000 votes and the election by 2,400 votes, and Mrs. Green, the Democrat nominee for GOP Homer Angell's seat, was elected to Congress from Multnomah County, riding on Neuberger's coattails.

Of significance: The United Register and Vote

Committee is still in operation and still possesses the invaluable union membership roster for the 1956 campaign.

A FINAL NOTE

Are the unions spending money on politics and if so, how much? The national CIO finances report for 1954 offers some evidence. For the first time in years the CIO had to dip into its reserves $200,722 because its expenditures on a national basis exceeded its income . . . The CIO attributes the deficit to expenses for "heavier organizational, public relations and legislative activities"—meaning politics.

THE DEMOCRAT INCREASE

The following table reveals the extent of the Democrat increase in votes:

	1950	1954	Net gain over '50 in votes	Percentage	
Total vote for Democratic congressional candidates	19,987,000	22,281,000	+2,294,000	49.5	52.3
Total vote for Republican congressional candidates	19,738,000	20,096,000	+ 358,000	48.9	47.2

(Note: Percentages in right hand corner do not include 1.6 percent for third party nominee in 1950 and 0.5 percent in 1954.

132

GOP FAILURE TO MATCH DEMOCRAT VOTE INCREASE

The GOP failure to match the vote increase as compared with 1950 is best illustrated by the following table which shows some of the most notable failures by states:

State	1954 Democrat congressional vote, plus or minus, as compared to 1950 totals	1954 Republican congressional vote, plus or minus, as compared to 1950 totals	1954 Democrat gain over 1950	Electoral vote
California	+510,800	+122,600	+388,200	32
Delaware	+ 22,900	− 9,000	− 31,900	3
Illinois	+ 19,000	−271,000	+290,000	27
Indiana	+ 13,000	− 9,800	+ 22,800	13
Iowa	+ 26,500	− 95,100	+ 42,800	10
Massachusetts	+ 26,500	− 95,100	¦ 121,600	16
Michigan	+152,600	+117,600	+ 35,000	20
Minnesota	+126,400	− 7,600	+134,000	11
New Jersey	−172,600	+ 44,700	+127,900	16
Oregon	+ 55,000	+ 19,000	+ 37,000	6
Pennsylvania	+192,800	− 9,900	+202,700	32
Wisconsin	+ 71,500	− 40,300	+111,800	12
			Total	198

OREGON AN EXAMPLE OF GOP FAILURE

Of course there is no single set of reasons for the GOP failure which applies to all of the above states. However, Multnomah County in the State of Oregon —previously examined to illustrate labor's role in the 1954 election—also provides a sample of Republican failure. It is worth examining in detail—

133

The defeat of Senator Gordon would not have occurred had it not been for the failure of the Republican organization in Multnomah County. The simplest way to state the failure is as follows: 78.4 percent of all registered Democrats voted; only 65.6 percent of all registered Republicans voted. In actual count, 43,000 registered Republicans never went to the polls at all.

But the failure in Multnomah County went far beyond the fall in voter turnout. There are 815 precincts in Multnomah County. Under Oregon law, precinct leaders are appointed by the county chairman of each party, a man and a woman who are co-equal and co-leaders. On election day the Republican party organization was short 730 of the necessary 1630 precinct leaders in Multnomah County.

The law also provides that the county registrar appoint Republican and Democrat poll watchers from nominees submitted by the county chairman, and that he name an election board at each election precinct composed of an equal number of Republicans and Democrats. It has been traditional practice that the nominees for election boards be supplied by the county chairman. On election day the GOP lacked 600 poll watchers, and on the election boards in many precincts there were no Republicans at all. Oregon law provides that in addition to poll watchers, board members have the right to challenge votes. In the forenoon of election day, approximately five hours after the polls had opened, it was discovered that the GOP board members had not been briefed on their rights and a flying squadron was sent around the community to inform them.

134

This failure to man the polls becomes doubly significant when the following is related. On the Friday before the election, the Gordon-McCall organization sent out a personal three-cent letter to every one of the 140,000 registered Democrats. The Friday after the election the Post Office advised that out of the 140,000 first-class letters sent, 22,000 had been returned marked "Addressee cannot be located." This superficial evidence of fraud in Multnomah County makes it clear that had Republicans had ample poll watchers and election board members and had they been properly briefed, probably several thousand Democrat votes would have been thrown out, which spelled Neuberger's margin of victory.

. . . It is clearly evident that the Republican party was out-maneuvered, out-manned and out-financed in the 1954 campaign. This essentially must be attributed to organized labor, not the Democrat party.

It is likewise plain that labor now intends to make politics co-equal with its other principal activities and that 1954 is only an indication of what is to come.

America, for forty years, has been witnessing a decline in the power of party organization. This dates back to the popular election of U. S. Senators, the decline in the power of the Speaker of the House, the decline in patronage and the growth of "independent," or "voting-for-the-man-rather-than-the-party" movements. Party organizations have largely become "volunteer" bands of public-spirited citizens, with apparently only limited numbers and a limited amount of energy available. They can be moved by adverse circumstances which result in the "crusade" type of

135

campaign, but, without reward, little else moves them.
. . . Labor can provide political workers and organizers trained far better than any political organization ever offered at any time. Labor uses volunteers but it does not depend on them. And, most important, organized labor demands that its adherents vote the straight ticket—meaning the Democrat ticket.

A reflection of this entire transformation is to be found in a letter from a precinct committeeman of 35 years' experience in St. Louis, Missouri, and a relatively prominent attorney, who wrote after the 1954 election:

"If we are to have a two-party system of government, there must be political patronage. If this absolute truism is ignored, then a party must rely upon the magic of its leader's name—in this case, President Eisenhower. That magic is not enough to secure victory. It is of great help, of course, but it does not take care of the fringe situations—the one-vote-a-precinct tasks.

"Any person who is expected to do the most important job of all, 'get-out-the-vote,' is entitled to prime consideration. Our precinct people have now grown old in battle and, because their important work is unrewarded, recruiting of the young and energetic is impossible—he goes to the Democrats, where partisan politics is still understood. Every four years our ranks are enlarged somewhat by enthusiastic workers, such as the Willkie enthusiasts or the Eisenhower rooters, but inevitably their enthusiasm is destroyed by the total ignoring of reward for the faithful.

"My opponent, the Democratic committeeman of my ward, carries his ward with the help of 43 political jobs he as a Democrat can win for them. Although the Republican party nationally is in power, not one job has been given to a worker in my ward and, as far as I know, none in any other.

"Consequently, our best men go to the Democrats, where they are rewarded with the jobs and I don't blame them. Our concern is always for the big shots. The candidate when elected gets the job—the precinct worker gets nothing. Never when our party is in power do we think of anyone in the lower echelon . . .

"In St. Louis we sponsored a Nixon dinner. I personally sold twenty-nine $100 tickets to my friends. Yet, on election day, not one cent was available for the precinct workers in my ward, who are the grass roots of a political party. Our city chairman has resigned in disgust.

"No help has been given to the precinct worker during this Administration. You won't have him for the next election. Television, radio, etc. will never replace the precinct captain and his workers, and the sooner the higher-ups realize it the better.

"The Republican businessman (so careful of his cash) and the political leaders seem to expect the workingman to fight the battle for big business. They expect from him a political enthusiasm not shared by the former. They expect him to work without thought of reward or goal. Well, they are wrong . . .

"I have been proposed as chairman of the Republican City Central Committee (to fill the vacancy by resignation). I wouldn't take the job under present conditions under any circumstances. Perhaps our men at the top should read 'American Parties and

Elections' by Howard R. Penniman of the Department of Political Science at Yale University, page 388.
"I am amazed that I have taken valuable time to write this letter. I expect no results whatsoever."

If the Republican party is realistic in its appraisal of the future, it must realize certain facts of life: (a) that some of the causes of the decline in party organization—popular election of Senators, decline of the power of the Speaker and elaborate Civil Service safeguards—are here to stay; (b) that something can be done to halt the promotion of "independent" voting if we want to do it; (c) that unless we devise new incentives, no great dependence can be placed on "volunteer" worker type of political structure; and (d) that the only truly effective political instruments are now in the hands of labor leaders . . .

What can be done about it?

VI

CAN ANYTHING BE DONE ABOUT LABOR?

Organized labor's success in getting out the vote for the Democrats in the congressional elections of 1954 became almost an obsession with Humphreys because he saw no way the Republican party ever could match labor's well-financed, highly-professional campaign machine. He did not have much faith in volunteer workers, since they were moved only by great issues or charismatic men, and these did not come along every campaign year. And, though he believed the Eisenhower Administration could do more to rebuild the Republican organization by using its power of patronage, he recognized that Civil Service had greatly weakened this power.

His solution was to attempt to separate the leaders of labor politically from the rank and file. Humphreys believed in labor unions as economic organizations and he did not want to weaken them economically. What he sought was to convince union workers the

Republican party felt this way so they would not automatically vote Democratic.

He constantly bombarded the White House and the Republican National Committee with his ideas. Much to his despair, although they agreed with him, they did almost nothing about it. The conclusion he eventually reached was that most Republicans could not help thinking of labor as they, a different breed of men, and, for that reason, workers could not identify with the GOP. He would not have been surprised by what happened in 1968, when, according to a Gallup poll, a last-minute shift gave 56 percent of the union vote to Hubert H. Humphrey, while Nixon ended up with only 29 percent.

There are numerous memos in Humphreys' files on what the Republican party should do about the labor vote. One, dated December 9, 1955, was the subject of a meeting in Sherman Adams' office in the White House the following day, at which Len Hall and Secretary of Labor James Mitchell also were present. A notation in Humphreys' handwriting indicates that everyone at the meeting approved the memo.

Entitled "Plan to Meet the Problem of Labor Leader Activity," it read:

ROLE OF ADMINISTRATION

1. The President, in some appropriate form (special message to Congress, TV appearance, or otherwise) makes a comprehensive statement as to what the Administration has done for LABOR and to advance the strength of labor unions.

2. All Administrative officials would continue to treat labor as the important segment of American life it is, with full sympathy so far as proper collective bargaining, benefits, rights, etc. are concerned (if some healthy innovations could be offered, all the better).

3. The Executive Branch in its utterances would make direct appeals to rank-and-file labor, with particular stress on the economic health and the welfare of the laboring man under the Eisenhower Administration.

4. Extensive plans should be made for real Labor Day celebrations, with the party and independent groups keeping step in their preparation.

ROLE OF PARTY

1. Must expound what the Eisenhower Administration and the Republican party are doing to advance the economic betterment and general welfare of the rank-and-file members and to provide opportunities for the development of strong unions.

2. Must appeal directly to rank-and-file members to be loyal to their unions, but to oppose efforts by union leaders who have become politicians to deprive rank-and-file members of their freedom of political action.

3. Must establish channels of communication to rank-and-file members by organizing rank-and-file committees across the nation and launching auxiliary drives by Women's and Young Republicans' groups to gain unionist members.

4. Must persuade a sizable number of states to

elect a representative number of labor unionists as delegates or alternates to the 1956 Republican National Convention.

5. Must, without the participation of Administration officials, identify and attack the political activities of union leaders that circumscribe the political freedom of rank-and-file members.

6. Must, without the participation of Administration officials, identify and attack the socialist philosophy of left-wing union leaders who have become politicians, as epitomized by Walter Reuther.

ROLE OF INDEPENDENT GROUPS

1. Independent unionist political freedom committees should be set up.

2. Committees for union wives should be established.

3. Intellectual groups should be organized to promote and produce articles, news stories and resolutions on the over-all issue of political freedom in unions.

TIMING

1. Administration, party and affiliate efforts through December, January and February *and from then on* should be concentrated on a direct appeal to the rank-and-file membership.

2. A special labor message to Congress, probably in February, might:

a. establish a definite pro-labor philosophy so far as legitimate unionism is concerned, with special emphasis on protection of political freedom of individual unionists.

b. propose Taft-Hartley revision

c. offer innovations for strengthening union structure and/or worker benefits.

3. In March, to help establish party "line," a magazine article, written by person identified with the official party structure (not government), should set forth the problem in terms of *political* activity of union leaders using union funds and union prestige.

4. The article should be followed by a full scale effort by party spokesmen to educate the public on the unusual political role labor leaders are assuming and the extreme philosophy they are expounding.

5. In May, on the presumption that, meantime, considerable numbers of rank-and-file committees would have been set up on a local basis, there should be a national tabulation of this achievement and an announced decision reached on how to further organize for the campaign.

6. For the August Party Convention special attention should be given unionist delegates and alternates and a rank-and-file unionist advisory group should be invited to attend the Convention.

7. In September an all-out Labor Day celebration.

8. In September and October prominent roles should be given unionist speakers in the campaign (appearance with candidates on platforms, trains, TV shows, etc.), rank-and-file delegations should visit White House, candidates' headquarters, etc., and the entire rank-and-file enrollment program stepped up until election day.

143

CONCLUSION

A year of study of this problem has produced the conviction that a real penetration of the rank and file can be achieved and there are strong indications that if it progresses sufficiently a number of top labor leaders, now distressed by the ambition and left-wing philosophy of the Reuther leadership, would split off from it and possibly shift to the Republicans. In addition, it has been evident for many months that the 1956 campaign must develop a burning issue to be successful. Quiet sampling and other experimental moves during this year of study make it clear that the above plan would provide the issue—political freedom!

Throughout the 1956 campaign, Humphreys kept pressing for action on labor. In a memorandum to Adams dated October 26, he proposed that President Eisenhower hold a White House meeting with rank-and-file representatives to dramatize the fact that he was not anti-union. He had it all worked out down to how to get picture coverage in the newspapers and on television. The memo reads:

Here is our proposal for a rank-and-file meeting with President Eisenhower:
1. By telephone, we have determined that we can have from one to three automobile loads of rank-and-file union members, paying their own way and losing a day's pay to do it, come to Washington to visit the

President and confer with him. The states to be represented would be: West Virginia, Maryland (Baltimore and Hagerstown), Pennsylvania (McKeesport, Sharon and Scranton), Delaware, New Jersey and New York —a total of about fifty people.

2. Their automobiles would converge outside of Washington approximately two hours before the appointed hour, be decorated with banners, and drive around the White House for the benefit of photographers, etc.

3. Possibly somebody can think of a better publicity method of handling this, but here is our proposal: The President would greet them on the back lawn, with TV newsreels, photographers and press in attendance. Bert Collins, a shop steward from Scranton in Walter Reuther's UAW, would be the spokesman for the group. He would tell the President very quickly the number of unions represented, the number of states, and would give him a two or three sentence estimate of how much of the rank-and-file vote he is going to get. We would hope the President would respond with a minute or so of remarks. Nearby we would have standing Ed McCarthy of Rhode Island, the rank-and-filer who seconded his nomination at San Francisco so the President could recognize him and shake hands.

That would be all. It should not take more than fifteen minutes out of the President's day, if that much.

4. Every one of these people would be a rank-and-file unionist, with none having any higher ranking than Collins as shop steward.

(Reason for selecting Collins: When Reuther heard

145

of Collins' effort in behalf of Eisenhower in the Scranton area, he sent an international organizer to Collins' local to have him ousted as shop steward. The union voted overwhelmingly for Collins and threw the international organizer out instead.)

We need to be given a day and an hour so that we can start telephoning these people, as the whole project will take quite a lot of organizing.

Humphreys even attempted to enlist the Women's Division of the Republican National Committee in his campaign to drive a political wedge between the union leaders and the rank and file. He devoted a whole speech on the subject to a meeting of women party workers, saying in part:

The days of the old-time political machine are gone. They were dead for us by 1932. They have been dying on the Democrats for the last ten or fifteen years. It is very difficult today to point to any community in this country and say that there is a well-organized neighborhood in either political party. . . .

There is just one exception to this picture. The closest thing to the old-time political machine today . . . is organized labor as represented by the labor leaders . . .

What is the solution?

First, I would like to remind this audience that this Administration has demonstrated not once but a thousand times that it is a friend of organized labor. I would like to point out to you that this was not only productive so far as organized labor was concerned

146

but was productive in 1956 when, according to several substantial surveys, it was shown after the election that the rank-and-file labor vote increased nine percentage points for President Eisenhower and Vice-President Nixon.

I would remind you that the Achilles' heel in the present picture is the fact that most of the labor leaders—not all of them but most of the labor leaders—spend union dues and voluntary contributions without the consent of the rank and file.

I think we have the greatest opportunity in the world in that fact, in that Achilles' heel. That is the point on which they are vulnerable.

I would like to urge you to go back home and make sure that a survey is taken in your state, in your county, in your city, and make it as wide as your influence spreads, to determine how many precinct workers you now have who are members of unions. I am talking about Republican political workers. We tried to get several states to do that in 1956. They were amazed to find out how many union members they had among their precinct workers and they did not even know it.

I will give you the happy result in New Jersey. Out of 7,500 precinct workers surveyed by the New Jersey State Central Committee, 700 were members of unions, or approximately ten percent. Now, that is a nucleus of a labor organization right there already inside the party. I think if you made this survey, and I don't care what part of the country you are from, you are going to be surprised how many union members are already out on the firing line for us.

147

I don't want to let this moment go without saying to you that the greatest error the Republican party could ever make would be to alienate the rank and file of the labor people. Let us not do it. Fight the labor boss, if he is wrong, but remember the man with the votes is the workingman and that is your business —getting votes. Don't overlook this huge pool of votes.

I would like to suggest something else to you . . . COPE, Committee on Political Education, which is the official political action arm of the AFL-CIO, has a highly organized drive on to win over the working wives and the union wives. Don't let them outbid us. Don't let them out-organize us. These wives are just as anxious to get into politics with us as they are the Democrat party, if you can make it attractive enough to them, and I suggest that you do that.

. . . Our greatest problem today is the recruitment of volunteer workers. I cannot state it strongly enough. I think every program you devise has got to be devised that way, with that in mind. That has got to be its purpose, how to get more people working in the precincts, how to get more people doing the basic political jobs that have to be done . . .

VII

THE BUSINESSMAN
AS POLITICIAN

The Republican party traditionally has been regarded as the party of business; but to Humphreys, businessmen in politics were a constant disappointment. Unlike the leaders of the AFL-CIO, he found, most of them have no understanding of politics, of how to appeal to people; in fact, he frequently remarked, "most of them don't like people." They feel they have done enough when they contribute money to a campaign; the work of getting out the vote is beneath them.

Humphreys also resented the fact that many businessmen feel that politics—and politicians—are beneath them.

He expressed his attitude in a memorandum he prepared for Len Hall on July 7, 1959. Entitled "Material for Off-Record Speech to Businessmen," it read:

You are going to build your remarks around these points:

149

HANDICAPS

1. Businessmen have an inordinate suspicion of politicians, believing that they cannot be trusted, that they are tricky, that they will double-cross you, dip their hand in the till, etc. I have been in the business and political worlds for thirty or more years, and I think that if I had to choose between the two as to which had the more integrity, I would lean toward the politicians. The first rule in politics is that when you give your word, you keep it.

2. Businessmen think that the use of money will solve all their political problems; that they don't need to participate beyond that point. They have the idea that contributions control votes. Naturally, there is some element of truth in this, but it is basically fallacious. (Make point that as a congressman, you have seen a couple of longhand letters from farmers that have had more influence than telephone calls from big contributors.) Businessmen should drop the idea that they can "buy" their way. It can't be done.

3. The belief of businessmen that "politics needs business methods" is one of the great fallacies that keeps businessmen disillusioned with politics. Suppose politicians started saying that "business needs political methods." The basic difference between the two is simple—in ideas, ideals, philosophies and ways of life. Business deals in matters that can be weighed, measured, felt and sometimes eaten. Frequently they can be given engineering tests: tensile strength can be tested, vertical and horizontal pressure resistance

150

measured, density taken, rust resistance noted, porosity gauged, etc. etc. You can calculate a cost and a profit. In politics, you can't even calculate the costs.

4. Because of the fundamental difference between business and politics, businessmen tend to be impatient with the endless bowing to protocol that goes on in politics. A businessman may make a major decision without consulting anyone or, at the most, two or three of his associates. In politics, it is not an infrequent thing to consult a half dozen or a dozen people. You may not even want their opinions, but they have to "be consulted," not "be told." More overriding among businessmen is the feeling that they must start at the top in politics. Left to our own devices, we would all be generals, and there would be no privates. For some strange reason, everybody thinks they are authorities on politics. And when it comes to this kind of thinking, businessmen top the list—most of them are certain they would make master political strategists overnight. I have seen one or two who would, just as I have seen one or two politicians who would make corporation presidents overnight, but on the whole, whether the businessman enters the politician's field, or the politician enters the businessman's field, each had better start at the bottom and work his way up. This basic impatience and lack of the understanding of human relations within politics causes businessmen to be failures in politics.

5. Probably the most difficult thing in politics for businessmen to grasp is the lack of a "chain of authority." The chain exists in politics, but seldom the authority. Businessmen cannot understand why the Re-

publican National Chairman can't "order" something done. They envision him as a board chairman of a great sprawling organization matching the power of an auto magnate in Detroit whose mere snap of the fingers may change all the advertising in the windows of 5,000 automobile agencies. There is a basic difference in the relationship between the Detroit auto magnate and the local dealer on the one hand, and the Republican National Chairman and, say, a ward leader in your town. The dealer is directly dependent upon the board chairman for his livelihood. Your ward leader would starve if he depended upon the Republican National Chairman for a livelihood. You must remember that most of the people in politics are volunteers and get nothing financial out of it. (Explain the disappearance of patronage, rise of civil service, elimination of caucus, reduction in powers of speakers, growth of independent voting, etc., have all combined to weaken political chain of authority to point of nonexistence.)

ADVANTAGES

1. Businessmen have been trained to organize—people, things, events, even thoughts. This is a great advantage in politics, where organizing ability is more and more difficult to find. A great weakness in political organization is the tendency to try to do too many things. In other words, there is lack of selectivity in projects to undertake. The organized mind calculates the probabilities of achieving something, and, of

course, this is particularly true of the businessman.

2. A businessman is trained to keep records; most politicians hate even to make a note. Yet records are absolutely essential to basic precinct work and scores of other operations connected with politics. There is no such thing as a well trained precinct organization that does not have records on all the voters. These take time to compile and a great deal of time to keep current.

3. The businessman has been trained to make decisions. People who are not used to making decisions often make bad ones and usually find it an ordeal to make any. Politics definitely could use more people who can make decisions, but I would remind you that I've stressed that businessmen frequently must learn the protocol of decision-making in politics.

4. One of the greatest assets that the businessman brings to politics is knowledge of "follow-through." To state it in contrary terms, the greatest single weakness in politics today is lack of follow-through. People in politics start something; they almost never finish it. If I were going to advise a young businessman how to get into politics the quickest, I would suggest to him that he specialize in finishing things that politicians have started.

5. Business people are usually taught to train people. Since politics depends on volunteers, which means beginners and amateurs, the lack of training systems in politics is appalling. There isn't any question about it; politics needs training courses, and businessmen could supply them once they got going.

OPPORTUNITIES FOR BUSINESSMEN

1. If I were a businessman and I wanted to be a real power in my community, I would start out doing precinct work tomorrow. I think if I had the ordinary wits and organizational and executive ability of most businessmen, I would control the political scene within three years. This would not be true everywhere, but it would be true in nine out of ten communities. In the tenth community, this hypothetical businessman would have plenty of recognition at the end of the three years, even if he did not control.

2. Considering less than fifty percent of our eligible voters usually even bother to vote, plus the fact that only a mere sliver of the population even helps work in politics, do you wonder that we get bad government in many areas? After the 1948 elections, polls were taken inside the Republican party. We found [that] an appalling number of professional and business people did not make a practice of voting. Of the group surveyed, the only businessmen who showed any civic interest, as measured by their voting record, were invariably members of Kiwanis, Rotary or Lions Clubs. On the whole, the record showed a disgraceful lack of interest by business people. Fortunately today there is an effort to try to remedy this. It's high time. I wish I could say that organized labor did not drive you to it, but organized labor did.

I think I have made it rather clear that the field is wide open for businessmen in politics, but actually I don't have sufficient words to impress on you the woe-

154

ful lack of manpower in our political parties today. You hear talk about block workers. Don't kid yourself. You could get all the block workers in this country in a small high school football stadium. They simply don't exist any more, except on paper. But they are absolutely essential to a real political organization. Businessmen could do a great deal toward setting up block organizations, contributing to both the manpower and know-how pools.

Now you have the opportunity to make up for your own deficiencies. You've got all of the assets, the training and the ability to do a superlative job; in fact, a better job than anyone else. Will you do it?

Humphreys had a plan for organizing businessmen to set up "block organizations, contributing to both manpower and know-how pools." He had outlined it two years earlier in a memorandum to Meade Alcorn dated April 1, 1957. It was, in effect, a plan for setting up what Humphreys called "corollary political organizations." The memorandum read:

Subject: Small Business Division

GOALS

There is no doubt that a properly-run Republican small business organization could produce effective results if it applied itself to the proper goals. Those goals should be:

1. Raising money.

155

2. Development of precinct work by employer and employees.

Under present conditions it would probably both be helpful to the party and to small business if a third point were added: interest in legislation. But this should not be incorporated without consultation with the White House. However, the organization would grow much more rapidly and probably produce far greater results if the legislation were one of the stated goals, because it would give them a real feeling of self-interest. Its inclusion is urged.

ORGANIZATION

The small business committees could be set up in either one of the two fashions: (1) operating within the Republican National Committee structure, with the states actually doing the work (which is the system used for our Labor Division), or (2) as a semi-autonomous organization with its director operating from the Republican National Committee in the same fashion that the Federated Women and the Young Republicans do. While the first choice gives the Republican National Committee more thorough and complete control as compared to the second, there are advantages which can be gained by adoption of the second choice. Among them are: (a) a complete national-state-county organization could be set up with chairmen heading each unit (people like to have titles and it promotes *esprit de corps*), (b) the clubs would probably raise a great deal more money if operating

156

as a quasi-independent organization, (c) the groups would probably attract many more members than if made part of the regular organization and would have greater appeal to Independents and Democrats, (d) clubs thereby would provide a stepping stone for people to enter the Republican party, (e) in campaign years when the $3 million limitation pinches, the clubs could help finance campaign activities, such as television shows, and (f) the organization would provide a more effective propaganda outlet (the Republican party is woefully short of corollary organizations compared to the Democrat party). The disadvantages of a quasi-independent organization are obvious: Not always controllable and occasional resentment by state and local leaders. But I think the advantages more than offset the disadvantages. If set up within the Republican National Committee structure, it is recommended that the organizational pattern be along the same lines as those in the Nationalities, Farm and Labor Divisions—i.e., a director (and a secretary) who works through state organizations attempting to get them to establish a counterpart setup. This means that the National Committee act as a catalyst, stimulating the formation of small business groups much as we set up rank-and-file labor committees. While this method is much slower and less spectacular, it unquestionably avoids headaches.

PERSONNEL

From everything that we have in our files and on the basis of other information, Don Sigerson of Oak-

157

land, California, sounds like the man to head the operation, whether quasi-independent or within the Republican National Committee structure. It is his idea, he made it work in California, and he believes in it. Those are three invaluable ingredients.

In his own literature in the California operation, he bluntly urged employers to try to influence their employes. It is suggested that this recommendation be omitted at the national level. He also asked employers to distribute literature in their plants, which likewise should be omitted at the national level. With these two exceptions, the above recommendations are not out of line with Sigerson's own program.

PUBLICITY

It is recommended that there be no publicity about the formation of this small business operation until the skeleton organization is set up, at least at the state level. Then it is urged that the program be announced by the President's participation (perhaps the leaders could call on him at the White House, etc.). We followed this method with the Labor Division and it proved very successful and seemed to get us far more publicity than had we announced our plans before we achieved some of them.

VIII

DON'T FORGET
THE FARMER

*No one votes his pocketbook more conscientiously
than does the American farmer. Even in this age of
television, the farmer leads a relatively remote life.
Such issues as civil rights, crime in the streets, urban
decay, air pollution, crowded airports, downtown traffic jams do not touch him personally. What does affect
him is the price of wheat.*

*Harry S Truman proved this in 1948. He carried
the Midwest—and won the election—largely by convincing the farmer the Republicans were responsible
for the drop in farm prices. Humphreys did not expect
Mr. Truman's victory, but it did not surprise him. He
had been worried by Thomas E. Dewey's failure to
answer President Truman on the question of farm
prices, more than once referring to Dewey as "that
dairy farmer in the homburg."*

*From the moment President Eisenhower took of-
fice, Humphreys kept bombarding the White House
with memoranda on the importance of the farm vote*

159

and how to keep it—namely, by thinking always of the farmer's pocketbook.

In a typical memorandum, undated but clearly written in 1953, Humphreys listed thirteen points which, he thought, should be kept in mind by the Administration in preparation for the 1954 congressional elections. The first point reads:

We have to do something about the price of eggs. This is killing us with the rural and farm wives all over the country. Everybody knows that any rural or farm wife depends on her "egg money." And if it isn't as good as it was, *she* is sore and the whole family hears about it and the whole neighborhood. We are literally being murdered at this time by the refusal of the Department [of Agriculture] to do anything. I think [Defense Secretary] Charlie Wilson and Harold Stassen should be told to buy a two-year supply of eggs if necessary—anything to bring the price up.

The thirteenth point reads:

Now I want to finish as I began. God damn it, somebody has got to do something about the price of eggs and I don't care what the budget figures are or anything else. I say buy them and I say do whatever is necessary to get them bought.

In a memorandum to Sherman Adams, dated March 14, 1957, Humphreys wrote:

I am advised (and I think accurately) that within

160

an hour of the defeat of the corn bill last night in the House telegrams went to 171 of the 245 drought counties in Texas extending drought relief for another thirty days. (It has to be renewed every thirty days or it automatically ceases.)

This leaves 74 counties cut off from drought relief in Texas at a very unpropitious moment from our standpoint. To make it worse, five of the six counties in the district of Congressman Bob Poage (who led the fight against the corn bill) are cut off from an extension and I am told that on a map it looks like a gerrymandering job since on three sides of Poage's district are counties immediately adjacent which will continue under the relief program.

Inasmuch as these telegrams went out last night to the individual counties, the other 74 could go out to-night with every chance that it would solve the dilemma, but let it go another few hours and it will probably be in the newspapers with adverse effects on the electorate.

I am advised that there has been some rain and improvement in Texas but nothing that could yet be called ideal. Perhaps this move is justified but even if it is, its timing is not particularly good.

Humphreys had statistical proof that his concern for the farmers' pocketbook was politically justified. In a memorandum to Meade Alcorn, dated April 30, 1957, he wrote:

Subject: Decline in President's plurality in farm counties

161

With Secretary [of Agriculture Ezra Taft] Benson persisting in unloading surplus corn on the market (thus cutting the price of corn, causing feeding of pigs which in election year 1958 will cause a sizable drop in the price of hogs) and with the announcement of the 22 cent drop in the support of wheat, I think you should take a cold look at what this kind of policy did to the President's great popularity in the last election since it will give you some idea of things to come next year. The figures are startling.

Below are listed 267 counties in which at least fifty percent of the population actually lives on farms in eleven states which are most basically affected.

50% Counties		No. showing decline compared to 1952	Average decline
Illinois	9	9	— 2.4
Minnesota	32	32	— 6.7
South Dakota	33	33	— 3.3
Kansas	17	17	— 4.9
Wisconsin	16	16	— 7.0
North Dakota	28	28	— 14.3
Montana	12	12	— 10.3
Colorado	3	3	— 6.2
Iowa	29	29	— 8.5
Missouri	45	39	— 3.3
Nebraska	43	43	— 7.2
Totals	267	261	— 7.6

IX

ON THE QUESTION
OF PATRONAGE

*Humphreys was a party man. He did on rare occasions
vote for a Democrat, but those occasions were extremely rare. Usually, he voted even for Republicans
he detested, and it was a matter of principle with him.
He believed in the two-party system. Those who
boasted, "I voted for the man, not the party," simply
pained him, for this, he believed, could lead only to
political disarray, the kind of situation Richard M.
Nixon had to face when he entered the White House
on January 20, 1969, with both houses of Congress
technically in the hands of the Democrats—and both
parties split.*

*Significantly, he chose his friends in the Democratic
party without regard to whether they were conserva-
tives or liberals. One of his closest Democratic friends
was the late Maury Maverick of Texas, a militant liberal. Others included James A. Farley and the late
Edward J. Flynn of the Bronx. They all had one thing
in common: Like Humphreys, they were party men.*

163

Humphreys realized, of course, that it was idle to hope to recreate a disciplined two-party system in the U. S. The erosion of the powers of the Speaker of the House, the growth of the civil service system, and the New Deal welfare programs alone had made that impossible. However, the White House still had vast powers to make the Republican party a cohesive force, he kept pointing out. Civil Service had not completely destroyed the power of patronage.

Humphreys wrote innumerable memoranda on this subject. Several of them were letters prepared for Len Hall to submit to President Eisenhower. The copies in Humphreys' files, for some reason, are undated. One of them, a detailed call for "a thorough reevaluation of the Administration's political operations," reads in part:

The first questions raised [by Republican national, state and county committeemen] are in the area of patronage. The questions go to only one segment of the patronage problem. Patronage is much more than the desire of a Congressman to put a constituent in a job. Much of our trouble comes from the tendency of appointing officers, without political experience, to think that patronage is merely the demand of the faithful (most of them incompetent) for a reward for political services.

It's that, plus many other things, including:

1. The fact that the promise of a change cannot be fulfilled unless people are placed in jobs way down the line.

2. This Administration cannot command policy

and cannot be secure from political sabotage unless it has men who share its philosophy way down the line. It can't even know whether or not it has loyalty or whether or not changes are needed unless it puts new men in down the line. The head of a large organization can't run it, or even evaluate its policies unless he has men of his outlook at all points at which facts are evaluated and recommendations made. Otherwise, he's operating in a vacuum. He can't possibly control policy and judge facts on all the things that converge on him. He represents only a token change. The old policies and attitudes prevail.

3. Democratic appointees, coming out of local Democratic party organizations, and given the cloak of Civil Service protection, still represent this Administration. This is embarrassing to local Republican leaders and Congressmen. The local public deals with the same Democratic politicians. To them there has been no change. To them it is manifest that the local Congressman does not have enough influence with his own party in power to get the changes made.

4. Democrats and New Dealers embedded in the lower reaches of the Federal Government still use Federal patronage to bring in people of their philosophy and loyal to them politically. They will use their positions to do small favors at the behest of the Democratic party organization.

5. The failure to spot Republicans down the line in the agencies deprives us of the long awaited opportunity to develop and train in government young people with our philosophy. We are not building as we should. We are not giving fair representation to the

millions of people who vote our philosophy. Many of them, in honest opposition to the Fair Deal Government, would not take government service. Now that we have a government which they can honestly support, they are still locked out. The work of this Administration will not have permanent impact unless we develop new men, at all echelons, in government service.

The public is acutely aware of most of these implications. People know that we cannot deliver on our promise of a change unless we change personnel. We cannot properly reevaluate old policy and generate new policy unless we have new people taking a new look at the problem and opportunities at all levels.

Now, what about the Civil Service? We agree that we want to preserve the career Civil Service. We must recognize that the Democrats, by screening and selection, filled the Civil Service primarily with Democrats. We know that the momentum of this process is still running. We can document clear-cut cases in which Civil Service rules have been rigged to keep Republicans out and bring Democrats in. We know that recommendations from Democratic Congressmen will in some places help a candidate for Civil Service appointment while a letter from a Republican Congressman will handicap him. This will continue until we have Republican representation at all major hiring points. This can be done without, in any way, injuring the Civil Service structure. The Democrats had a political man sitting alongside of every personnel man who was not himself a political appointee. Fifty (50)

166

men would protect us throughout the Government from having Civil Service used against us.

We must dissent from the opinion of the Civil Service Commission that some 700 positions are enough to control the policy of an organization of over 2,000,-000. It is manifestly impossible for one man to control the policy and evaluate the facts in an organization of 3,000. Yet that is the ratio of policy jobs as the Civil Service Commission now sees it.

It may well be proper for the Civil Service Commission to take such a position. Its primary responsibility is to protect the status of career employees; political appointees frozen in by the Democrats as well as those who qualified by meeting bona fide Civil Service tests. But the decision as to where the Administration needs its own men to carry out its policy and to deliver on its promises cannot be left to the Civil Service Commission.

There is grave concern in many quarters as to whether the bureaucracy has not grown so big and so powerful that the people have lost their power to control their Government. If, in voting a change, the people can eliminate only .03 percent of their servants and must keep the remaining 99.97 percent, how responsive is the Government to the people and how deeply are the people in bondage to a permanent bureaucracy?

Before the election, the general estimate was that it would take 5,000 new officials to effectively take over the Government. After election, the management firm, McKinsey & Co., made a survey which pinpointed

167

1,500 policy forming jobs essential to the control of the Government. The Civil Service Commission now cuts that in half.

In numbers, the demands of the Republican state organizations and Congressmen for jobs is a drop in the bucket. Five thousand jobs would satisfy every known demand. That is about one quarter of one percent of Federal personnel. Normal turnover by death and leaving the service will be twenty (20) times that. We haven't put as many Republicans in the Federal Government on organization recommendations as the 1,400 we have eliminated as security risks. This preposterous state of affairs exists because most of the key personnel spots are still manned by Democrats who are not supervised or checked in any effective way by Republicans.

[I suggest] that we document the cases in which a Congressman wants a man placed, and show the incumbent, his politics and his Civil Service status. It is entirely impossible for us to litigate individual cases. There must be the will to make changes. We must be satisfied that there are in key appointing spots and in personnel offices, people who will try to make changes that are desirable. We now have people who will try to find reasons for not making changes and they smother the agency chiefs in technicalities. If we can't replace these personnel men, we must put a man in with each of them. The political organization and the Congressmen must be satisfied that they will get a fair break inside. Then they must leave what happens to the judgment of the agency. They haven't the time or the personnel to process and litigate individual cases.

Fifty political men in spots where they could watch the selection of personnel, such as the Democrats had, would smooth the operations of a government, its philosophy and its public relations at a cost amounting to about one millionth of the Federal budget. For the party organization to do it would break the bank. Moreover it can only be done effectively and smoothly as an inside operation—the Administration delivering on the change it promised in the campaign.

With these men inside the agencies, normal turnover and replacement would provide the change. As it is, normal turnover and replacement work against us.

The personnel change promised during the campaign can never be delivered as long as Civil Service refuses to recognize as policy makers the regional directors who are the agency to much of the public, the personnel men who mold the agency and the public relations men who speak for the agency. Who can build or remodel an agency if he cannot choose his chieftains on the firing line in the field or the man who selects and trains his personnel or even his own mouthpiece? And, how better to hamstring or sabotage a man than to leave these vital organs in the hands of people who oppose his aims?

To effect these changes need not impair the career service one little bit. The anti-Republicans in policy jobs involve less than a fraction of one percent of Federal personnel. Many of them could be shifted to other jobs where they would not impede or embarrass this Administration. It would relieve our embarrassment with the public if we merely changed faces in local

169

and regional offices still bossed by well-known Democratic politicians.

One final point on patronage. We need a unified command and don't have it. When a man is appointed on political recommendations, he's hardly in his office before some of the White House staff are pressing personnel on him without regard to political channels and sometimes without regard to political party . . .

On this last point, there is another memorandum in Humphreys' files. It, too, was a letter prepared for Len Hall for submission to President Eisenhower. It begins:

Mr. President, I think the major problems facing us today include not only party organization in the selling of the Eisenhower program, but also the proper handling of patronage. What I am about to say, I would say regardless of who was chairman—

If party organization is to be successfully promoted, and if the patronage is to operate smoothly, it is necessary that it operate strictly through the party machinery.

People in politics want answers. They want somebody they can go to and get answers; they want somebody that they can look to for answers. The success of all political organization is the centering of the patronage disposal in as tight a unit as possible. In the picture today, the logical man to have the say in patronage and to deal directly with the President is the National Chairman. If it isn't the National Chairman, those in the organization and the others down through the ranks soon have a complete lack of respect for him because he cannot deliver on anything. The operation just doesn't work successfully if somebody stands between the Chairman and the President. When that is the case, the politicians quickly learn to bypass the Chairman, since he hasn't any say anyway, and to go to the man who stands between the Chairman and the President. It is the old business of the shortest distance between two points is a straight line.

Then there is a second possibility where the patronage is handled by the President and the Chairman. I refer to the practice which worked so successfully under President Roosevelt and Jim Farley. If you had two powerful factions inside a state, Roosevelt would play with one faction and Farley with the other. If excuses had to be made, Roosevelt would say, "Well, Jim wanted it that way and I couldn't do anything about it," or Jim would say, "The President wanted it that way and I couldn't do anything about it." The result was that both factions got some recognition and their support could be obtained by either the President or the Chairman when the moment came when it was needed . . .

In still another memorandum on the subject of patronage, Humphreys summed up:

. . . It boils down to this:

1. Patronage is more than jobs; it concerns policy, political prestige; our campaign promises, security from political sabotage.

171

2. It can't be handled on a case by case basis, with a litigation about each job.

3. We haven't placed as many people from Republican organization channels as we have eliminated as security risks.

4. The known patronage demand could be satisfied with 5,000 jobs. Yet there is a normal turnover of 20,000 a month in the Government.

5. The best intentions on the part of agency heads will accomplish very little. We will get nothing but dissatisfaction until we can effectively insist that a representative of this Administration sit in each key personnel office.

6. That's how the Democrats did it and are still doing it. The selection of people for replacement needs, Civil Service and non-Civil Service, is now being used against us. We must have Republican representation within the personnel operation of government if this Administration is to develop young men with its philosophy. Otherwise we have no long term meaning.

7. The Civil Service Commission position that there are only 750 policy-making jobs in the Federal Government is untenable. It means that the people can change .03 percent of their public servants and must keep 99.97 percent. The Civil Service Commission fails to accept as policy jobs regional directors who are the agency to the public, personnel directors who mold the agency, and public relations directors who speak for it . . .

172

X

WELCOMES HOME
DON'T JUST HAPPEN

"Fifteen thousand people greetea us wnen we arriveu at the National Airport the next morning. President Eisenhower put protocol aside to meet Mrs. Nixon and me at the airport. He was accompanied by the entire Cabinet. The Democratic as well as the Republican leadership of the Congress was there. Several large groups of Latin American students studying in the Washington area also were on hand, carrying placards of a very different nature from those we had seen . . . for every unfriendly face we saw in Latin America we saw a thousand friendly ones."

The quotation is from Richard M. Nixon's book, Six Crises. *He was describing the reception that greeted him when he returned from his visit to Latin America in 1958. He had gone there originally to attend the inauguration of Arturo Frondizi as President of Argentina. His return had been plagued by Communists. The worst incident of all had occurred in Caracas, where he and Mrs. Nixon were attacked by a mob that wanted to kill them, a mob shouting* "Muera Nixon, Muera Nixon." *Death to Nixon, death to Nixon. Under any circumstances, his welcome home would have been a warm one, but welcomes home don't just happen. They may look spontaneous on television, but they must be organized. On May 16, 1958, Humphreys wrote a letter to Mr. Nixon telling him just how the reception which pleased him so much at the National Airport was organized.*

It reads:

CONFIDENTIAL NOTE
Dear Dick:

A man likes to know who his real friends are and that is the purpose of this note to you.

The idea for an airport reception for you started last Friday morning before you went to Venezuela and an enormous amount of work was done before the Caracas "incident." Needless to say, what had started as a reasonably good bonfire was turned overnight into a roaring conflagration by the reports from Caracas. Here are the names of the people who did the organized spade work and a brief description of the nature of what they did:

> *George Hart,* Chairman of the Republican District Committee: Sent out 5,000 letters, hired buses, got us buses free (note below), helped provide police escorts for buses, and above all else was responsible for getting the *Star* to run its front-page editorial demanding a Government-workers holiday (the *Post* turned him down on the same idea).

174

Ray Dickey, Washington attorney: He did a splendid job in voluntarily organizing college campus groups, working with college presidents, student councils, etc., paid for six buses out of his own pocket, even painted signs in his own basement himself, helped contact such people as Bishop Hannan, etc.

Bishop Philip M. Hannan: He had to work by indirection but there is every evidence that he put forth an extensive effort at Georgetown and Catholic Universities.

Dr. Warner Lawson, Howard University: Responsible for the Howard University ROTC band.

Abbott Washburn, USIA: Did a tremendous job lining up groups, including Northwestern Senior High School championship band, helped on Howard University student groups and band, etc.; also gave us considerable direction on what the signs should say.

Catherine Gibson, President of Women's Federation: Had her shop start a phone campaign to the District, Maryland and Virginia Republican Women's Clubs.

Val Washington: He and his office worked on producing young Negroes and Negro students.

Clancy Adamy and his Patronage Division staff: Made phone calls to every Republican member of the Senate and House in the name of Meade Alcorn (on a speaking tour) urging them to release their office staffs and to attend the airport reception themselves.

Vera Ash: Did an excellent job of personal contact with radio and TV commentators 24 hours in advance of event to help build crowd without making it look partisan.

Meade Alcorn, Bertha Adkins and Ab Hermann: One hundred percent behind the whole idea.

Representative Leslie Arends, House GOP Whip: Put out "whip" notices to all GOP members and worked like a beaver to get Democrat members to the airport.

Harry Brookshire, House Minority Clerk: Set up all details on getting House members and staffs to airport.

Gib Garrison (Miller of New York), of Bull Elephants: He organized telephone drive on office staffs to go to airport.

Robert Williams (Beamer of Indiana), of Bull Elephants and Young Republicans: Teamed with Garrison on above and also worked on college campus effort.

Don Tubridy (Republican Congressional Committee), President of District of Columbia YR's: Put together two bus loads of YR's and worked nearly all night with other volunteers on assembling signs on sticks and later distributed them at the airport.

Lee Wade, Republican Congressional Committee Air Director: He and two assistants worked two days and one night making ninety signs supplied above.

Jack MacKenzie (HEW): Organized telephone campaign to junior executives in Government urging them to go to the airport.

Victor Johnson: Worked with Senate leaders and Administrative Assistants Association in producing Senate office staffs.

176

James Gleason (Knowland of California): As president of the Administrative Assistants Association, handled phone campaign to produce Senate staffs.

Mark Trice (Minority Secretary of the Senate): Organized the trip of the Senators to the airport.

Edward Colladay, former National Committeeman of District of Columbia: As counsel of D. C. Transit Company, obtained ten D. C. Transit buses gratis to transport members of the House and their staffs to airport.

Commissioner Robert E. McLaughlin: Voluntarily got into the act, ordered a holiday for District workers, and had the Fire Department "Welcome Ladders" put out.

Governor Adams, General Persons, Tom Stephens and Art Minnich, of the White House: All pitched in in promotion effort and Governor Adams was particularly cooperative at all times and, of course, contributed greatly to the final decisions.

Last but probably first was the cool-headed and diplomatic handling of the whole thing by Charlie McWhorter, your office, who was besieged by people yet managed to get their efforts channeled into the right grooves, while he touched all bases. What impressed me most was that he was always available on the phone which showed me he had things well organized so far as your office was concerned. It was really a pleasure and a comfort to do business with him.

Supplemental to the enormous enthusiasm and the electric atmosphere of the occasion the orderly work

177

of these people produced ten bus loads from the House side, five bus loads from the Senate side, two bus loads from D. C. Young Republicans, one bus load of D. C. GOP women, two bus loads of National Committee staff, one bus load from George Washington University, four bus loads from Georgetown University, five bus loads from Catholic University including one bus load of nuns, one bus load from American University, four bus loads from the University of Maryland, three bus loads carrying the Northwestern High School championship band of Hyattsville (arranged by Michael Ronca, Appleton 7-7400), two bus loads of Howard University ROTC band (arranged by Lawson, organized by Captain McDonald, Assistant Professor of Air Science), three bus loads of Suitland Maryland Senior High School band (arranged by Mr. Lally, Redwood 5-6400) and ninety signs in Spanish and English.

Need I tell you that everybody did this without any thought more than their country and their admiration for Dick Nixon. The spirit was terrific and what you and Pat did deserves every bit of it. I know it was a tremendous and frightening ordeal at times but it was a great thing for this country and it certainly should awaken the world concerning political conditions in South America, while at the same time opening the eyes of many sleeping Americans as to the quality of leadership they elected in 1952 and reelected in 1956.

XI

THE ANATOMY OF
THE GOP

Election day 1958 was a dismal day for the Republican party. No one, least of all Humphreys, had expected the GOP to regain control of the Congress, for, if they hadn't managed to win control in 1956 while Eisenhower was crushing Stevenson, how could they now? In the Senate races, victory was a statistical impossibility as everyone in the party (except Eisenhower) had admitted from the first. Of the 34 races only thirteen were for seats held by Democrats; six of these were in the South and in the other seven all the Democratic candidates were incumbents. Quite aside from that, the nation was in a mild recession. Unemployment had risen. And so had prices and taxes.

Granting this, as every Republican leader (again except for Eisenhower) did, no one had anticipated the extent of the Republican defeat on Election Day '56. The Associated Press called it "the worst licking the GOP has taken in years." As James Reston wrote in The New York Times, *it "confronted President Ei-*

179

senhower with the largest Democratic majorities in the House and Senate since the days of the New Deal."

Len Hall called Humphreys to ask: How come? What was the matter with the Republican party that it could suffer such a defeat even with the most popular President since Franklin D. Roosevelt in the White House?

Humphreys' answer, dated December 31, 1958, was a devastating criticism of the Republican party. The GOP was bound to lose except in extraordinary times or with an extraordinary candidate like Eisenhower, he wrote, because it had become an exclusive club of middle-class WASPs. The WASP middle class were in the minority in the U. S., he pointed out, and for that reason the GOP, by choice, had become a minority party.

Along with his diagnosis, Humphreys offered a remedy, one which time and circumstance slowly have been forcing on the Republicans. Heading his memorandum to Hall, "Subject: The Party Image," he said:

. . . Ray Moley and I once put together a book on politics (but by mutual agreement withdrew it from the publisher and it has never been printed). I always thought my greatest single contribution to that book was this formula: All the voter wants to know is, are you interested in *him?*

When you start from that premise the best you can say for the Republican party today is: The Republican party is interested in *him* in an indirect sort of way— it thinks that what is best for *him* is a balanced budget,

180

decentralization of government, states' rights, civil rights and a sound dollar. He may agree with every one of these points but you don't convince him without the warm human appeal to him in terms that he understands—not in the abstractions listed in the preceding sentence.

Let me give you an example of what I mean. If I were a punch operator on a production line and belonged to the United Auto Workers, why would I think you were interested in me if the only people I ever saw you with were Red Curtice, Charlie Wilson, Henry Ford and Tex Colbert?

Or take the matter of governmental appointments. As a die puncher, I read the newspapers and all I see is another retired corporation executive going to work for the Government or being called in as a consultant. I seldom see a unionist or a little guy or even a small businessman in the picture. Then I turn the page and read a statement by a Democrat spokesman who says the Republican party is the "party of big business." I simply ain't got much reason to disagree, so I accept the idea and I'll probably vote Democrat at each and every opportunity.

I ask you! Have you ever in your life tried to be friendly with the people who show very little inclination to be friendly with you? It is that simple.

Now, when you add to this picture the tirades of not a few Republicans against organized labor, what is there left for Mr. Punch Operator but further proof for a conclusion he already has reached.

Is it any wonder that when Joe Bachelder took a

poll for us after the 1956 election he "discovered" that the people in fifteen of sixteen widely dispersed congressional districts regard the Republican party as the "Party of Big Business" and the Democrat party as the "Party of the Little Man"? The label is on us completely, indelibly, and forever unless we do something fundamental about it.

What are we going to do about it?

As you know, I have preached for years that the whole picture can be changed without so much as supporting one radical piece of legislation. It is simply a matter of attitude, of self-expression, of posture or whatever you want to call it . . .

Point: It is the fact that the Republican party *is* the party of big business because it is run by people from the big business world.

The answer: Obviously you have to change the people running the party; you do not eliminate men from the business world; you dilute them and their influence by broadening the base.

This, we have not done, nor is there any indication we intend to do it.

If the overwhelming percentage of our appointees to top Federal jobs are from the business world, you can expect these appointees to think, "Is this good for business?" and they speak in those terms, not, "Will this make more jobs?" not, "What will this do for the Italian-Americans?" not, "What will this do for our Negro people?" not, "What will this do for a Polish-American?" not, "How will this affect labor unionists?" not, "What will this do to the little fellow?"

Point: We simply must have in the Federal Government and in the high party councils a far greater representation of people who think in these various terms, *or the party itself will never think in them.*

Such a move would change the associations of all of us. George Humphrey associates with big businessmen because he does not know anybody else. He is not to blame. George Meany seldom associates with anybody but labor unionists. He is not to blame, either. It is his way of life.

But a political party not big enough for both George Humphrey and George Meany isn't going to be a winning party. And the Republican party is simply not that big at this reading.

You have heard me say a hundred times: "Why don't we say *our* labor unions?" You know why we don't say it as well as I do. Because most Republicans regard labor unions as their enemies. They think they belong to the Democrats. What a welcome mat!

People wonder why the farmers don't like Benson. I see no mystery in it. Most of his associates are meat packers, processors, implement manufacturers, etc. These people are not farmers. They live off the sweat of farmers. The hierarchy in the Agriculture Department actually said to us during the '54 campaign: "Yes, eggs are only twelve cents a dozen," and then they added hopefully, "And they have to go down some more before we can clean out the surplus." In other words, they are thinking in economic terms of what twelve cents per dozen will do to the market, instead of what twelve cents per dozen will do to the farm wife's egg money. Is it any wonder farmers say, "There is nothing much wrong with Benson's program, but we don't like him."

You will recall that after the '54 election I made a series of recommendations. Two of them are directly pertinent to this subject.

"6. . . . precinct workers point to a harmful and widespread opinion that the Administration and the Republican party are for "big business" and not "for the little men." The following proposal is designed to help overcome this handicap and, at the same time, serve as a corollary to the proposed appeal to the rank-and-file of labor.

"*Recommendation:* It is proposed that the Republican National Committee establish a 'Human Interest Shop' to cull thousands of newspapers and other publications daily across the country for human interest incidents, where the principal party or parties would merit recognition by mail or otherwise from (a) the President, (b) the White House, (c) the Vice-President, (d) a Cabinet member, (e) a Senator, (f) a member of the House. The letters, of course, would be released to the press, radio and TV at suitable levels."

"7. The President's stag dinners have created considerable attention and are rapidly taking on an institutional aspect. The guests have, for the most part, been very prominent people, together with personal friends of the President. The following proposal might add to their political attractiveness, without distracting from the President's personal enjoyment.

184

"Recommendation: It is proposed that frequent 'human interest' personalities who have performed reputably or heroically be included at dinners and that other White House 'little men' events be held from time to time. The 'Human Interest Shop' proposed above could be the source for singling out these people."

The above two recommendations were nothing more than a set of actions to demonstrate our interest in individuals, in plain ordinary people. But let's take that proposition further.

How many labor unionists did we have for candidates in 1958? I know of only one—a chap from Gary who ran for Congress in the First District of Indiana. How many Polish-Americans, how many Italian-Americans, how many Jews? You can count them on one hand.

When you go to a Republican dinner, whom do you see at the head table? It is an even money bet that the head table will be 100 percent white, Nordic, Protestant, upper income class.

Who gets introduced from the audience? Ditto above.

How many Catholics on the Republican National Committee? Maybe one, maybe three, maybe five— we don't know. How many Italian-Americans? One. How many Polish-Americans? None. How many Jews? One. How many Negroes? Two (both from Mississippi). How many labor unionists? One.

In the overwhelming majority of states this same set of questions applied to the state committees will produce the same set of answers.

Point: The unescapable conclusion is that *a cross section of the Republican party is a mere splinter in breadth compared to a cross section of America.*

In reaching a solution to this problem one of the major handicaps which will be met is: The typical attitude of Republicans who agree that all the foregoing is correct and that something should be done about it is, "yes, *but.*"

Reason: They are disciples of what I call "association with aloofness."

For example, how many Republicans do you know who have sat down with a group of rank-and-file labor people and talked it out? I have done it repeatedly and I know how much fun it is and results can be gotten. But it is worth your life to try to get most Republicans to do it. How many Republicans would sit down in their own home and break bread with a Negro? I've done it, but even I don't say much about it for fear other Republicans would look down their noses at me. How long would you last on Long Island if you started associating with Italian-Americans? You know the answer and so do I. But the fact remains that until the Republicans *themselves* change this attitude of "association with aloofness" and introduce the real juices of warm friendship, we will not be able to become the majority party again.

In conclusion, I would point out to you a case history you know much better than anyone else: Teddy Roosevelt. The Republican party as a majority party began to die when he died. It had its chance for recovery with President Eisenhower, but the wrong people helped pick the personnel and set the tone. Ike alone would have done far better.

I don't know what can be done between now and 1960, but it will never be done by tiptoeing through the tulip bed. Somebody has to speak out in the forthright manner that Teddy Roosevelt employed. Who will it be?